Abused Ac

Abused Academics

International Handbook for University Dwellers

Dr Rudolph Desmond Parkinson

iv

To

Foreword

People around you encourage you to go to university. It was the same with the school; if you study hard, you will have a better job and a bright future, and it is good to be literate. While they all are and were probably right, it is time for someone to speak up from a different perspective. Going through the school/university pathways may not be the only way to the literacy. Attending academia can make or push people to become illiterate.

'Pragmatic Illiteracy' is probably the most significant knowledge problem that our world faces right now. Firstly, we do not read, and if we do read, we do not write; the unutilised literacy skills make us illiterate. Secondly, we know how to read and write; however, we have no idea what to read or write and how. Practically, we are illiterate.

This problem has been rooted deeply in academia. In terms of education, the schools and the universities have a sole purpose: to teach the students how to think. The outcome of thinking is something new; it could be completely new or an update to what already exists. If we think and think and get nowhere new, it is a concern; we may not know how to think. Simply, academia has failed us.

Incapability in thinking is so serious that now we barely could find thinkers in academia. Without thinking skills, academics are vulnerable to abuse. We see lecturers and researchers who follow others' thoughts and teach students what other people's thoughts were; we make academics be followers rather than leaders. At the same time, some noticed the thinking void and started filling the gap through thinking on people's behalf. Businesses, religious organisations, and media are three good examples of those who have successfully dominated the world of 'proxy thinking'. Even academics fail to think. An academic career is the only career in which you are expected to work for free while people abuse and exchange your labour for money.

I will mention some of the common ways academics – from students to professors – are being abused. I raised the alarm that the universities' function is shifting towards being a business, a religion, or a media. Academic freedom and freedom of thinking and speech and expression were the reasons that, at some point in history, academia pushed human society forward. It seems we are losing the battle to those who have more money, more power, and more control because of living in a capitalist world.

In this book, I feel committed to informing the audience that the university should no longer be an obvious option. Both students and staffs need to rethink before entering, staying, or leaving the university. The function of the university has changed, but people keep coming and staying in a highly deceptive re-purposed academia. These people expose themselves to unnecessary abuse, which is hurting individuals and our society.

People join the universities following their dream and finding a way towards independence in their lives and changing the world and pushing it towards being a better place for all; however, they soon find themselves doing tasks that have nothing to do with the world or their dream. While they know they are stuck, they do not attempt to change the current situation. They usually 'think' that staying in an abusive but predictable and survivable situation is better than starting an unpredictable but happy and healthy pathway. This way of thinking is referred to as Abused-Abuser Relationship that usually continues when Abused think about leaving their Abusers and starting a new life; however, they find it scary and risky for several reasons: this is the only thing that they are good/skilled at; they have been kept safe with this relationship, and it is predictable; their background will make it impossible to find another job that pays the bills; they know no one outside their relationship to help them; most of the jobs will ask for a recommendation letter from references who are the previous employers.

If you stay open-minded, you will find that many academics, whether student or professor, are in a similar situation. Lack of thinking keeps their guard down to abusers who sell the people's youth, skills, and the best years of life to earn money.

I try to look at academia from a fresh perspective, which results from free-thinking and academic freedom outside the academia, and it is not welcome inside the academia. I could not share my real name to keep my students and academic colleagues safe from more abuse; please do not share it if you know my name. To keep my identity hidden, I could not ask an editor to check my words, so I apologise if the language does not fit the purpose and the text has been written in a hurry. I attempted to keep the text readable and straightforward for a wider audience; each chapter is small and independent to make it easier for selective reading. As a result, some repetitions were unavoidable. I welcome your comments through this email, the only official communication channel related to this book: RudolphDesmondParkinson@gmail.com

Disclaimers

- The information presented in this book should not be associated with a specific university.
- The claims made in this book may not be accurate or generalisable to all the universities.
- This book is to help people and support them in their decisions.
- The information in this book should not be taken as advice.
- Reading this book will take a few hours of your life, a few hours that you will never get back. Please make sure you are happy with it.
- The information and knowledge are solely the author's opinions and do not reflect those of their previous, current, or future employers.
- This book may have permanent effects and side effects on the reader, and you may not think the same after reading this book. The reader's discretion is advised.
- The author is not responsible for the consequences of using this information.

Table of Contents

Chapter 1: Elsa Says: "Let it go"

When you love something, there will always be people who would use your love, interest, and care to abuse you. Some of us love academia. Such love may have started from the first children book or movies and cartoons or school library and joy of learning, but it never stops. One reason is that we are biased in our thinking. If you spend more time, energy, and money on something, it becomes harder to let it go even though at some point it may harm you. The good examples are a failed business or research project, a long-term relationship without life satisfaction, a money pit car or house, and a career in academia. It has a name: Sunk Cost. Therefore, the Vietnam war and the Concorde project continued. We are optimistic that we will win with the next lottery ticket, we will win the war, and we will get promoted next year.

It is not just the time you have spent but the quality of the time that you have spent too. You spend the best years of your life in schools and universities. Your best memories are from there, and you never can repeat them. Some nostalgia addicts arrange a reunion party, trying to have another taste of what they used to have. Whenever you think of those days, nostalgia tickles your nerves, and your conditioned brain sends pulses to your lips to smile and laugh with joy. The same pulse that tells Pavlov's dogs to salivate with the clicking metronome.

You want those good old days back like a good dog.

Academia is also friendlier than many other businesses. The people read books and seem or pretend to be civilised; they believe that all human beings and natural beings are equal. Even if they do not believe this in heart and soul, they act like they are not discriminating against people. It is a good feeling to be in such a civilised environment. Can you find a better business than academia for work? It is probably the perfect dreamland for people with certain calm and relaxing personalities who are tired of imperfections of the real world to shove the head in the sand.

If you are an experimentalist, you focus either on a single narrow aspect of a single problem and stay open-minded to find a solution or answer a single research question. You can control the confounding factors and run experiments and be systematic and clean and follow the protocols. You can never do this in the real world. If you are a social scientist or humanities, you can follow the existing research methods and create something new through observations, surveys, and interviews.

There is room for all to think, do, and write as long as it is based on their job description. Otherwise, the academics will have to do all that exciting part on their own time and at their own cost. You wonder why one joins academia then.

History tells us that scientific methods and logical reasoning won over prejudice, superstition, and emotional and reactive decisions. Science changed the world, and now it is science and technology that leads the way. A powerful country is the one that is ahead in the never-ending sci-tech race. To make decisions, the governments consult with scholars and scientists on evidence and commission them to do research and produce the evidence that makes the difference. Paradoxically, the academics themselves do not make decisions logically. Notably, the young ones are vulnerable to biases and fallacies that leaves them utterly vulnerable to abuse.

While academics think and produce evidence to make the world a better place, they ignore being logical in their career choice. They usually fail to make their own life better. On the other hand, and under the capitalist environment, the universities have turned into corporate profit-making organisations with no care or mercy for their students or staffs. They also have shifted from impactful work into a Hollywood-style business model of shows. Academia has become an unfair and abusive ecosystem and ruins lives, dreams, and the chance for having a better world. Regardless of all the abuse, the academics continue to follow the rules. Some would say a new renaissance is needed to reform academia. For such renaissance, we all need to be aware of the abuse to avoid them; even if we can plan to leave the academia, listen to Frozen's Elsa and let it go.

Chapter 2: Studentship's Sinking

In the old days, when there was no internet or no access to the internet, it made sense to attend the university because the books, journals, experts, and other resources were all stacked in there. Nowadays, you can learn almost anything online. Unless you require using costly equipment or need a qualification to practice your career (i.e. law and medicine), you do not need to attend the university.

Another reason for sending people to the university was that many universities were publicly funded, and education was free. It made sense to learn without spending money. It still does. On the other hand, the parents wanted to get rid of their beloved kids and kick their asses into independence. If you consider all the reasons together, you will notice that it does not make sense to go to university for many right now.

I start apologising to all the students who had to sit in my classes, who are currently sitting in my classes or will sit in my classes in the future. The educational system wants you to be in the same place at the same time and to receive the same information and expect you to learn. The system knows that you are different people, but it still wastes the most valuable part of your life, making you sit in these classes. This approach is the first abuse you face as a person affiliated with academia. Some of you deserve this punishment as you have nothing better to do; the others who have something better to do will find their ways out. The lecturers who understand will let you go. Why? Because you have already wasted your money coming to the university so why waste your time.

Entering the university, you expose yourself to be abused by the system in other ways too. If you want to be free in the future, study hard and study pragmatic books about life, getting a career, starting a business, and so on. Slides and notes are the worst alternatives to books and make you shallow thinkers. If you want to earn the foundation of knowledge, there are no shortcuts until the Matrix movie becomes a reality. Put your hopes on yourself, not on the name of your university nor your lecturer or in those slides.

The universities exist to suck your money and tell you what you can find for free online. If you leave out the exceptions such as medicine and law or the fields that require access to expensive lab equipment – when you have no choice but to get a degree – most of the other fields could be studied without attending the university. Steve Jobs and Bill Gates are only two of few examples of those who left the university for good.

I have seen people asking the experts in the field and university professors about how good their field of study is. They forget the bias in professors' reply. Of course, the existing high-level career holders will need you for slavery. For example, suppose no student goes to study in that field. In that case, the professors will lose their jobs simply because the university loves them and pays them because they generate income for the university through your pockets. In between, the government also provides financial support to keep you in its debts for decades, so you start and live your life in debt; on the other hand, because of having a degree, you will push yourself to get the highly paid job and pay more tax to the government. I would seriously suggest you rethink your future and update your thoughts every day. See if there is a way towards your financial freedom through learning skills and profession without attending a university.

Many students are aware of these issues, so they do not go to universities to learn; they are there to have fun and create unforgettable memories of their young ages hoping that Hollywood movies were telling the truth. They go to the university to experience an American Pie-style environment. It takes them three years to notice that it is not Hollywood or Hogwarts.

Last but not least, more and more employers are becoming more and more interested in skills rather than academic qualifications. It means those who can learn and use the skills within a year will always be ahead of those who attend courses and universities to get a degree within three years with no skills towards their career prospects. Of course, this is your concern only if you want to be employed; if you prefer to be your own boss, your road to independence is the hardest but with more excitement. Whatever you do, think unbiasedly before taking actions and always have monetary capital (rainy day saving) and social capital (support from family and friends) for penniless days.

Look at your personality to see if you are from the self-learning generation or from the lazy generation who would not move out of bed if it is not for attending school or work. See if you need a push of assignments and PowerPoint slides to learn, or you are a library and laptop person who can learn the most complicated science on their own.

Attending the university is an expensive and risky investment.

Chapter 3: Top-Ranked University of X

Universities rankings – similar to any other way of quantifying the quality – have their problems. The universities highlight their famous alumni and Nobel prize winners to give you the illusion that these people changed the world because they came to this university. You can easily name people who changed the world without even attending that university or any university at all. Who you become at the end has little to do with attending a university; it does, however, depend on who you are and how you spend your time/life. If you are looking for a piece of paper saying that you graduated or something like that, then the university is for you, but that piece of paper is all you will get no matter how top your university is.

The ranking systems are another way of ripping you off. Remember that you can get your chicken burger from McDonald's or Fleur. That will be your lunch, but they will cost very differently. Super leagues, Grammy's, Academy Awards, and Nobel Prize are all ways of ranking that decides who deserves the praise based on set and unset objective and subjective criteria. The criteria may not make sense and could be politically affected by those who have power and money. Those who set such rankings and awards are not public servants; the rankings are there for their benefits.

Each ranking system usually uses some similar and different criteria for putting a university's name higher than the others. These differences are there to show that each ranking system is unique. However, like a super league, it creates competition among the universities to get higher ranks based on those criteria. Some of these rankings are directly linked with the amount of funding a university gets and its enrolment rates. Commercially thinking, the universities are doing their best to get the higher ranks and stay there as long as they can. To do so, they invest their resources and direct their strategies towards those goals.

There are several university rankings, and it has become a profitable business to rank people, services, products, organisations, cities, and countries. Most of the websites now allow you to sort products, people, or universities based on several criteria. Since there are many choices, you need such tools to help you choose from among the options. You are simply confused, and these rankings are there to convince your confused self that one or two of these universities are the best for you. What matters is to realise that the criteria used by these ranking systems do not overlap with your criteria. For example, if you want a law degree and based on your best efforts, you only can afford to pay 50k in your currency for that degree, then your ranking system will be different. What you need to consider is that a higher rank would mean more costs for you. Does it mean quality? Does it mean job security in the future? You can never know until you spend that money. It is called a gamble.

Many say that I have never seen anyone unemployed when they graduate from the University of X. They all have well-paid jobs. I indeed suggest those many to read Thinking, Fast and Slow from Daniel Kahneman. This visibility bias is coming from several sources. Media advertise certain universities more than others. In news, movies, and TV series, you hear the name of certain universities more than the others; they prepare the ground for you to accept the lie. Another source of bias is the visible people; of course, successful people are more visible and are talking and showing off their success; it is more likely that you see them. The third source of bias is that the university itself does not lead to success: 1. Those who can afford to go to such universities are more likely to be from a wealthy or highly credited background, and that background supports them in their career as well; 2. If you go to the top universities, you and the people around you expect you to succeed. Such pressure would mean you will work your ass off to get that highly paid jobs. Your hard and smart work leads to success, not a magical spell of the name of a university. The fourth source of bias is the invisibility of the failed people. Remember that absence of evidence is not evidence of absence. Those who go to top universities and do not end up with a posh career are usually hiding from the news and social media. They fear that they will be blamed and constantly criticised for the failure because it must be their fault; everyone who graduates from the University of X is successful; give me one name who isn't!

One of my colleagues brought up that if you go to top universities, it is likely that you would know people who will be influential in the future, and such a network will guarantee your success. While I believe that if you look around, you will find some cases to prove this point; however, I also believe that any future success through any pathway involves several factors, including the country's economy, your personality, your field of study, and many more.

Chapter 4: An International University

You look at the university ads, and you see students from all colours and culture laughing on the green grass; the image that they want you to see and pay for to be in it. It must be an international university you judge based on the photos. No racism, all animals are equal, Orwell's right. You apply to the university and, as an international student, pay double, triple, or quadruple the tuition fee of a home student. That is not racism or nationalism. It is just what it is and should not be seen in those smile-filled photos. Those who pay double or triple do not receive more education or services. It is the same education and services, and they also pay more for rent, food, transportation, and visa. You also miss family, so you travel more often, or the family come to visit you. Without you, the university will fail. You and your family are a bank for the university and the government. Make everyone proud. Whenever you see the term international university, you should be able to translate it by now. Maybe the students in the photo were laughing at you.

That would be nice to get a piece of that picture. Still, you enter the university and realise that even though the university advertises diversity, the students behave like they are in their own country. They find a friendship circle from their own country or culture and stick to it. I asked a few of my Chinese undergraduate students why they are always together; it is an international university. They should take it as an opportunity. Their answers were convincing, and I should blame the international universities for not investing in the social aspects of education.

The main reason was that the new country looks strange to the international students, and they seek comfort with familiar surroundings: people, food, and culture. The university or the government that issues the visa for the student do not provide specific training for the students. Usually, the cultural differences, including food and entertainments, adds to the gap between home and international students. The second primary reason was the language barrier. Some of the students confessed that they never thought speaking English could be this hard, and they don't feel confident to speak with non-Chinese students; the majority of the international universities take it easy for international students and allows them to meet their English skills criteria after entering the university and not as a mandatory entrance criterion. The international students without academic English language skills sit in the same class as students born and raised in English-speaking families. A third reason is that there are more than the usual number of international students in some of the classes that add to the issue. In addition, many of these business-minded students think that there is no point in hanging out with others because when they return to China, they only need Chinese connections. The last reason is the fear of being judged. One of my students was brave enough to open up to me and explained that many people do not like Chinese citizens and still blame them for taking the major part of the world economy through breaking the intellectual property law – she mentioned the term copycat – and combining it with cheap labour. She added that they also think that all Chinese students who study in western countries are from a wealthy background, and the university accepts them because of their money; after all, they pay double or triple the home students. She explained that it is not true all the time. Many parents spend all their life savings on building a future for their children. The universities will expel them if they do not meet the entry criteria within a specific timeframe after entrance.

However, these are not the only issues. One of my lecturing colleagues said that it took him an hour to explain the final project expectations to his Chinese student in a one to one session. He was complaining that there are several things wrong. Firstly, he cannot allocate one hour to explain the assignment for each student; secondly, it is unfair to other students if he spends more time with one student because of the language barrier; thirdly, he sincerely believed that such students should not attend his class because they could not understand a single word that he says. He was surprised when a student used an app that scanned his paper and translated it into English; then he wrote the answer in the app in Chinese, and the app translated it into English. The answer was correct. As a final example, he said he was happy when his international student asked if he could record the session. Another home student explained that she is working for this international student and transcript the entire session and type it down in English. Then the student passes the English transcript to another student who translates it into Chinese; so he finally can read and understand the session. I found it a very costly and time-consuming approach and thought maybe the universities should use simultaneous translation headsets instead. My colleague added that having undergraduate international students with poor English is time-consuming, and he does not wonder why the university charges them more. Still, he did wonder why the university does not overpay the staffs who have to deal with these students.

The story is not specific to Chinese students. Many international universities now are attracting more students from countries that enjoy the wealth from Persian Gulf's oil. These students are not all from wealthy background, and some are using scholarships, but they also have similar experiences. There are certain differences between experience from Chinese students and Gulf students. Because of being an ally with the USA, most students from oil-based economies have much better English language skills. Some of these Gulf students are from conservative families who may travel with the students to the west; others prefer the education to be as remote as possible to stay with their families and study from their own country, without travelling and living in western culture. They also prefer postgraduate degrees compared to Chinese, who are dominant in undergraduate degrees.

Last but not least is that the students from the Gulf prefer to work on a final thesis that is relevant to the setting of their own country so they can work on it without attending the university. The challenge that my colleagues expressed about these students was that you could never be sure if it is them who works on the project or a paid outsourced researcher. Online temporary jobs platforms are filled with requests for writing dissertations and chapters, and you may not wonder about finding your own student's request among them. Indeed, some of them have no interest in learning or skills or the job market; they just want to be called a 'Doctor'.

Despite all these reasons, the international students are being treated as 'cash cows' or 'academic tourists', and there are no regulations to keep them safe from abuse. Usually, a country's policies and regulations apply to their citizens, and the university fees for international students have not been regulated in national policies. This legal hole allows the universities to compete and ask the students to pay the highest possible tuition fees. As long as there is demand from international students to study in the west, the tuition fees will stay high. This is the product fee they pay to hold a qualification from a prestigious university, just like those who can buy a bag for a few dollars from a local market or spend a fortune on a Birkin bag. It is time for international students to think either they want to learn or hold a Birkin bag. Within a capitalist world, the first-class seat costs three or four times of an economy seat on a plane, and you charge a tourist more than you charge local people. The students should remember it does not matter what university to get their degree from; at the end of the day, it is essential to know they have the skills for the job market. The time you spend in the classroom is not related to your future career, but it is time you spend outside the classroom learning on your own and learning new skills that will determine your future. You take the classes and deliver the assignments just to hold that bloody qualification. It will not mean you are qualified for the jobs.

It is not just the international students who come to an international university; the staffs come too. They usually apply for very expensive visas that usually will not be refunded by the universities. They have to extend and re-pay for this visa for between 4 and 12 years; the visa costs a fortune before becoming permanent residents or citizens. During this time, they will have to pay rent because the banks will not trust to lend them money to buy a property; in some cases, the banks may offer loans with the highest interests. The universities are aware and have special accommodations for staffs to make sure they will pay between 30-60% of their salary back to the university directly before entering their bank accounts.

Probably the worst disadvantage for these international staffs and students is the lack of knowledge. Whenever I speak to my international colleges, they always regret that they did not know what they learned years later. Many international people in the universities are anxious and stressed to deliver their tasks and assignments to secure their job and prove that they deserve the position. They only focus on their job or study and have no time for anything else. They also learn the culture through trial and error and lots of embarrassments. Unfortunately, the government does not provide any basic information about laws and regulations and rights; the university ignores them. It is only during the citizenship exam that they realise there is an app, or a book, or a website that they need to study and pass a citizenship test. Many Chinese students carry a large amount of cash with themselves, and students from oil-based economies wear pieces of jewellery and expensive clothing that make them a tempting target for criminals. The staffs are unaware of pension or tax regulations or the healthcare system and are too busy to find a cheaper accommodation while being ripped off by their employer on rent.

On the other hand, the university staffs have no idea how to communicate with international students or staffs. There are cultural, lifestyle, and political differences, and many try to stay on the safe side, which means no communication is better than any communication. The universities have no training on microaggression, and the staffs end up asking impolite and offensive questions such as 'where are you from?' and 'when will you get back?' which are simple questions for many but means you are a foreigner, do not feel comfortable here because you will get back. They say the question is out of curiosity. When an international staff gives an unexpected answer, the audience follows with 'sorry, where are you from?'. During pastoral care, one of my Chinese students said she has stopped communicating with all non-Chinese people after exposure to the questions such as: 'do you eat bats?'

Some of the universities have started courses on diversity and inclusion and unconscious bias; however, the contents of these workshops are general. Compared to media bombarding people with country-, religion-, and culture-specific stereotypes, the amount of training staffs receive is nothing. Some of the staffs are so biased that they should not be employed in an international university in the first place. You can see these staffs writing rude emails or yelling at international students on helpdesks which is not very helpful. An easy way to find out their biases is to give them the name of a country and ask them to give you the first three words that come into their minds. Stereotypes are the most accessible shortcuts for thinking used by media and politicians to divide and rule. Since thinking grey is the most challenging work in the world, people welcome such easy binary shortcuts.

Some of these staffs and student have been very defensive and started a hidden war. Extremism creates extremism. Similarly, in academia, I see the tribal approaches to employing, supervising, and sharing the opportunities. Some colleagues discriminate against students or employees based on protected characteristics (age, disability, gender reassignment, marriage and civil partnership, pregnancy and maternity, race, religion or belief, sex, and sexual orientation). Nationality and financial status are not among protected characteristics; accordingly, a penniless foreigner is a moving discrimination target. I have seen how friendly these staffs are to people with specific characteristics and how they consciously spend more time with them than others. They are trying to favour their tribe or take revenge for the historical or a single previous unpleasant experience. Many don't communicate or speak up, fearing being labelled as '-ist' word.

In some cases, it has no historical reasons. It is just a mafia or tribal management inherited and transferred from their original culture and fears (See LMIC chapter). You see that the departments or universities in a western country are filled with people from foreign nationals of one country in specific fields. With a quick chat with one of my colleagues from that nation, he highlighted that it is a cultural phenomenon, and they feel comfortable with each other and trust each other more than the others. He also said that he is a professor because of favours from the same nationals who included him in all the opportunities and networks. Because he is also part of the same network, he has to favour the students of those who helped him become a professor in the first place. This nationalism loop continues within the international universities. I have seen people from four continents, from low- to high-income countries, with this type of behaviour against the science's international and collaborative nature. It does not seem that the university has any control over this politics. At the same time, no one knows whether such practices are legal or ethical or if there should be a law to prevent them.

In summary, no one should be fooled by hearing the name of the international university.

Chapter 5: Doctor Doctor or PhD?

Y ou wake up one day and you 'feel' jealous of those called 'Doctor'. It is late for you to study medicine, and it is too expensive too, so it seems reasonable to go for a PhD. It is only three years, your life is worthless, and you have nothing better to do. I mean what you can do within three years except for joining a business or starting your own business and becoming financially independent and becoming your own boss. Being called a Doctor is way better. So, you spend your time on it and become passionate and convince yourself that this PhD is just right for you. Deep inside, you know it is not, and it is not in your area of interest, but you apply, and you get the funding, or maybe you are wealthy enough to pay in cash – so-called self-fund it. You are also surprised and happy, and you celebrate and open champagne for successful entry. When you start working with your supervisor, the entire topic of PhD changes and with it, your dreams collapse. Now, you should fit the square peg of PhD in your round hole. You stuck working on something that you don't love, but hey, you must show you are passionate, and you push the peg in yourself and believe that you are excited, and you are enjoying it. The peg becomes your life for three years, and you have nothing else to talk about because you have no life. Those who have a life or a plan for life do not apply for a PhD. If you apply for a PhD, it means that was the best of your plans. In other words, you had nothing better to do with your life. Call it a risky investment/gamble of three years of your life on an uncertain future.

Midway through the PhD, you will notice that the PhD candidate is a research fellow who gets paid half or one-third of a research fellow's salary. Then you learn about something called a PhD by publications or by published works or by special requirement or something like that. You can get a PhD by writing research and review papers without needing to waste three years of life on it. You can get a PhD alongside a full-time job. Sorry, you should have known better.

No matter how you get a PhD, never write 'PhD' after your name or signature because it results in less respect than the respect you get when you write Dr in the beginning. So, the rule is Dr at the beginning of your name is better than PhD at its end. The reason is that when you write 'Dr', it is not clear if you are a medical doctor (MD) or a PhD, and people tend to stay on the safe side and respect you like they respect a medical doctor until they find out that you are just another PhD that grows like a weed in academic fields.

Get a PhD by publications if you can; do not waste the best years of your life to do a research fellow's job for a third of a research fellow's salary. If you are in fields requiring expensive equipment to conduct research, you have no choice but to go with the flow and the peg; otherwise, choose the wiser way.

Chapter 6: The Classes of Academic Jobs

Many of those who attend the best years of their lives to the university classes also make their best memories in the university and always miss it. This happy experience is so joyful and addictive that many won't let it go. They become nostalgic and love to get back and get a bit more for that experience; master's and PhD are there to keep you a few more years, but it is not enough, is it? You need a job, a good job, an academic job. Whatever you do, nothing is going to be the same. Driven by nostalgia, you can stay in academia for the rest of your life and let academia penetrate in all aspects of your life and keep you distanced from the real world that you fear entering into it. If you have sat in the university classes, you will soon deal with other classes within the university: classes of jobs.

Your first jobs are not about your interest or expertise; it is about what money holders need. If you look at the description of academic jobs, you will notice no job titled Thinker or Game Changer or World Saver. They have a project, and they need someone to do it for them; your line manager is capable of doing your job, but they don't have time, so that is the only reason they need you; otherwise, you are not that special or unique job-wise. You need to pay the bills, so you apply regardless of all the facts. Of course, the job is irrelevant or slightly relevant to your background, but you tell yourself that it is your first job. You end up doing things that you don't like, but you have to do. Many are not lucky enough to get what they love, so they learn to love what they get. The discrimination between loving what you do and doing what you love fades away quickly, and you gradually learn to give up your dreams, accepting the reality that you need money. You even continue explaining to other people how lucky you were to get what you love, and many unfortunate ones have to love what they get. You will live with that guilt.

Soon you realise the burnout and try to change the job. It is the first time you notice that no one cared that you are leaving a job. The university just needs your notice on time to replace you. As Adele would say: 'never mind, I will find someone like you'. Since you are not from high-class jobs, it is straightforward to replace you.

There are three categories of jobs for you to apply for: 1. Administrative and Managerial or Professional Services; 2. Research and Teaching; and 3. Academic. The borders among these classes are not always visible.

The first ones are office jobs requiring coordinating tasks, managing people, organising meetings, doing the paperwork, and sending and receiving emails and mails. They usually do not require academic skills rather more people's and organisational skills. Since these jobs do not require high levels of skills, it is very common for the universities to ask the other job categories to do these jobs as an addition or as part of their original job description. These jobs are also very risky and less permanent. Whenever a university realises money problems, the contracts of these job holders is the first one that gets affected. The university does not use the terms such as being sacked or getting fired; the proper terminologies are 'end of contract' and 'risk of redundancy'. It is acceptable and routine for managers to see these staffs usually lose their jobs, and 'cut the admin costs' is a commonly used phrase in top-level meetings at the universities. When the university cuts such costs, the other job categories have to do the extra tasks. The admin jobs have no clear job descriptions and are subject to abuse frequently though performing extra tasks and being blamed for everything. The managers with less funding will ask the research and teaching staff to do the admin job family tasks. The universities are also OK to outsource or downsize IT department, which is usually listed among admin or professional services. I have worked closely with six universities, and my colleagues in all six universities at some point were unhappy about IT services. One of them said that the only thing that IT is good at is upgrading the system, which has one meaning: causing problems. Each update will cause enough problems that will take ten years to solve; if they upgrade the operating system four times, IT staffs will retire successfully. When I responded that I am using my laptop for work, he said I am lucky because IT is also good at purchasing a perfect laptop and making it secure by connecting to the university network so no one, not you, nor

IT, can log in to it. When you ask them that you need to use it at home, they say the laptop needs to get system updates by connecting to the university network; so, you have to bring them into the university for the updates or don't use it. He returned his laptop to IT and purchased one from his pocket, and lives happily ever after.

The second job class is more relevant to early career researchers, and the sub-levels of this category includes research and teaching assistants and then teaching and research fellows. You can apply and get these jobs with a graduate or postgraduate degree and start it with a fixed-term contract that usually gets extended depending on the funding availability. If there is no available funding, the universities encourage you to apply to similar jobs within the university and shift to a similar job or leave the university within a few months. These job holders usually work twice other job categories, and they are being referred to as early career researchers or 'postdocs'. Based on their job description, they get paid for a 9-to-5 job, but all in academia know that they work double or triple that time for free. Nature's survey of postdocs was eye-opening that this is not country-specific statistics. While the primary responsibility of these jobs is teaching a set course or research on set projects, the university encourages these job categories to grow and work harder and more to get funding or be active in a way that brings benefits to the university. If you can prove that you are bringing benefits to the university, the university will generously pay a bit of that benefit back to you as well. It is called 'promotion' and usually changes your job title to Senior Research Fellow or Assistant Professor or Lecturer or something like that. That's how you officially become 'academic'. Based on the current classification, you are not an 'academic' before this point despite conducting research and delivering teaching in academia.

The last job categories are more prone to change and are usually more permanent. At this level of the game, you will have no life. You just have to find money pots and beg them, supervise PhDs and master, teach all students, write and publish, collaborate and network, work in the lab on your research, edit and peer-review, and so on. You also have to line manage people from the other two categories, which will require training, supporting, and encouraging them.

It is a pyramid. While most jobs are administrative and easier to get, there are fewer jobs in research and teaching, and there is competition. Many who fail to find a job in these two categories leave academia and live happily ever after. Some of the second job categories stuck in that category until they retire and live happily ever after. The remaining people in the second job category don't let the academia go; they either get promoted or apply for another higher-level job which is a promotion. A low number of them succeed in promotion, but the 'hope' keeps many postdocs in these categories for years, if not decades; they benefit the university more than the other job categories. The universities provide training for them on how to work even more to get promoted and encourage them to keep applying for promotion next year or the year after or after a few years. Lower self-esteem and trying to prove that they are worthy will keep them going for a while. The intentional discrimination between the second and third job categories makes the second job family jealous and inferior, psychologically pushing them to work harder.

At some point, they realise the abuse and either leave the university or apply for a higher-level job and get it because of building their solid academic profile for years.

The academic job holders can relax because of more security. To discriminate, the university keeps the other job categories in open offices or shoves several people into one tiny office; however, the academic category gets an office to have privacy and focus and to invite people for meetings in their offices. Sometimes they are allowed to get a part-time or full-time secretary or admin because now they are too important to waste their time with paperwork. They need to find ways to bring money or students to the university or keep the current enrollment rate going. They also have to work overtime to design new courses, new course materials and curricula, read and comment on student projects, teach and research, apply to grants, manage people, and mark the assignments. They don't have to work as hard as the second category because now they have people who work for them.

Just like any other corporation, the universities follow a business model and predict the incomes and expenses. They usually do not wait for a course or project to fail and avoid the money drainage in advance. Keeping the current trends going is never beneficial for the universities, and the trend should continuously be increasing using more free resources and generating more income. When the number of enrolled students in a course is not enough, the affiliated lecturers are told to think about retiring. It is better to resign/retire with honour than being sacked. Of course, to make it look nice, the university will offer you an honorary or emeritus position which is unpaid and expects you to work for free. This position will prevent you from becoming homesick for your office, and you can occasionally come back to your comfort zone or die behind your desk like a loyal academic.

The bottom line is that the universities are heavens where people enter as students and exit as professors. It is just another corporation that tries to get you in with advertisement and in compliance with governmental regulations to get your money and give you a qualification. If you could learn the skills on your own, then the universities may employ you to generate benefit from you and pay part of the benefit back to you; if you can't or don't want to generate benefit for the university, then start your life with getting benefits for yourself, take your head out of the sand and look for the opportunities outside the university.

The universities have already noticed a significant number of their staffs and students are leaving unexpectedly. Some universities were worried about the financial loss caused by staffs' leaving and the bureaucratic employment and replacement process. Therefore, they started a procedure called "Exit Interview" during which they expect the leaving staffs to explain the reason for their leaving and their new jobs. Despite their nice try to collect intelligence on abused staffs, many never attend such interviews to confess for several reasons. The universities do not care about the leavers; the purpose of the interview is to benefit the university by keeping the abusable staffs.

On the other hand, you cannot complain about your colleagues or the university and document them; you may always cross-path. Instead of expressing your feelings, find a way to take revenge.

Chapter 7: Press Pressure

Publishing paper in a journal is one of the usual tasks that is expected from academics. Any time spent on the papers is directly and financially benefits the publishers. The university may benefit from the affiliation, and the researchers will have something on their CV. Unlike any other publication efforts in which the authors receive royalties from the publishers, the academic publishers pay nothing. The universities pay researchers, but they also pay the publishers to buy their journals' subscriptions. The publishers say that authoring is part of the researchers' job description, and their employers are paying them to write the papers. As a result, many universities, including those in low- and middle-income countries, have started publishing their own open access and free journals to stop costly publishing with commercial publishers. However, historically, some of the journals have built such a reputation that publishing with them could be an esteem indicator.

The researchers have to spend their time on research in labs and workshops or behind their computers and write the papers outside the working hours. Early career researchers or postdocs usually write the first draft of the paper; they usually work longer hours than any other academics and suffer from mental health issues. Job insecurity adds to their pressure. With the number of PhD graduates not matching the number of available opportunities worldwide, postdoc positions become more competitive and hard to get. When you get one, you do your best to keep and grow in it. If you change your jobs more frequently, it sends the wrong message to your next interviewer because you are more likely to change your job soon again, so they won't want you. It is pressure from all sides.

Writing manuscripts, revising the papers, replying to peer-review comments, modifying images to meet the journal's criteria, filling the forms, and submitting the paper and its one or several revisions is a time-consuming task. There is a joy in seeing a paper published, and I call it an 'academic orgasm', but it is addictive and could easily encourage and lead to academic abuse.

Another apparent problem with publishing a paper in a journal is the authorship issue. You can never know the actual contribution of each author to the paper. Leaving aside unethical practices such as guest and ghost authorships, it is unclear how many hours each researcher puts into the work. Some journals now have a section and ask for clarification, but the statement of contribution still is not enough or necessarily true and does not stop unethical practices.

Apart from that, many contribute to the paper but never make it to authorship or acknowledgements. It is also discouraging to do work for being acknowledged or ignored. If you are in academia, it is a daily routine to receive emailed requests to fill the surveys or participate in Delphi rounds or interviews or meetings. These are some of the popular ways of data collection in all experimental and social sciences. If you accept to help, you will spend time and receive nothing for that time. Those who have your data will publish and enjoy the possible benefits of the papers, and they may or may not thank you for contributing to the science. If you take that "thank you" emails to the promotion committee, they will laugh at you. In case of a survey, you get nothing; for interviews and Delphi rounds, you may get acknowledged, and again, if you take those acknowledgements to your line manager and ask for pay raise, they will blame you for wasting the time that they are paying you on something worthless, even though you might have done that extra work on your own time. It is another abuse to use people's time and data for your progress and paying nothing back. People should be compensated for their time.

The current authorship practice is flawed. It should change into contributorship so that hundreds and thousands of people could be listed as contributors with the level of their contribution at each stage. When the final report is ready, it is time for publication. The only option that all researchers think to have is the journals.

The journals are not quality gatekeepers, and peer-review itself may not be necessarily helpful. Three graduates of a tech institute released a program that put this hypothesis to test. They released a free web-based programme that writes computer science papers and includes graphs and citations: SCIgen - An Automatic CS Paper Generator. You only need to enter one or more fake author names and press the generate button to get a paper, an original contribution to science. The main idea was amusement, but the students and academics worldwide used it to generate and submit papers to journals and conferences. The known successful examples are on the website of this program, and it continues to reveal the scandal of peer-review for over 15 years. Some of the peer-reviewed journals that have accepted these non-sense papers are from top prestigious publishers and when the journal finds out, retract the paper. Peer-reviewed conferences were worse.

If it does not make you think, why not try using Generative Pre-trained Transformer 3 (GPT-3) to write papers for New York Times, poems, and computer programming codes. Your students finally will give you an essay that will get that A+. Publishers will be worried.

So if the journals are not that good and peer-review comments are subjective, and the entire publishing process is time-consuming, why aren't we shifting to a new model that excludes the journals and publishers as brokers between your work and your audience or your indexing database? Preprint servers are the future of publishing.

The publication itself could be the problem. We have millions of published papers globally; what is their impact except helping the journals' Impact Factors? The amount of time and money wasted in academia and through academia makes the entire publishing practice questionable. It is not just their money; it is, most of the times, public money. The ecosystem created for disseminating the research findings is not working. This ecosystem is to promote the universities and researchers through the number of citations and publications. Lay people or policymakers do not read academic journals. If the findings are not released in mass or social media in an understandable language and a usable format, they are useless. The published papers' uselessness is another reason why the traditional publishing industry fails and will continue to fail after decades of abuse and give back nothing valuable in return for time and money. We should discourage people from publishing in journals or with the publishers.

This story does not end well, I'm afraid. When I published my first paper in a subscription-based journal, I realised that I could not access my paper, and the publisher asks me to pay 90$ to download a copy of it. Of course, I had my submitted copy; the published copy only looked more beautiful; that beauty make-up is exchanged with the copyright of the paper, so I had no right to share that paper in any form with people. That was my first clue of the abuse. I contacted the university library, and they said they could order it, but it will cost me 15$ because it is not available through any of their network libraries. I contacted my colleagues in other universities, and they could not get it until a librarian who asked me never to reveal her name told me to use Sci-Hub. I got my paper in a second. I started research on it and found out about a documentary titled Paywall: The Business of Scholarship. Without any extra word, just find and watch it; it is not mine but would tell my story.

If you have something of value to publish, publish it as a book. Self-publish or publish it with a publisher that pays you over 50% of royalties.

Chapter 8: Closing the Doors to Open Access

Good for you if you are from the low- and middle-income countries (LMIC) because you have the choice to publish for free or with discounted fees in open access journals. I think any researcher who has no funding should be considered to be from low- and middle-income 'job' or 'setting'. But apparently, it is not the definition of low- and middle-income for these publishers. You write the papers for free; you may also research for free, you may write a commentary for free, peer-reviewers check your work for free, editors finally accept your work for free and then you must pay £3000 for the work done by free labour. As intelligent, abused professors, we have never noticed that this is the best way of modern slavery. The idea of open access started the wave of predatory journals that publish everything for a price.

At some point and about 30 years ago, physicists, computer scientists, and mathematicians finally found a solution for open science without abuse. They shared the free and public copies of their work in a preprint server before submitting it to the journal. Since it took and is still taking longer for other sciences to catch up, the publishers started Open Access schemes or scams for other fields such as medicine. To make them look lovely, we have green and gold open access. You can share your paper for free on preprint servers immediately and with no delay; why bother paying and publishing in open access journals? I tell you why because they have Impact Factor and get indexed in databases. If it makes you feel better, I must say that Impact Factor is no longer a valid evaluation indicator; many institutes and publishers have signed the Declaration on Research Assessment (DORA). Secondly, most of the top indexing database providers – following Google Scholar – have started indexing preprints which means your work will be visible. Choose wisely among open free access preprints, paid open access journals, or subscription-based journals.

With the emergence of pre- and post-publication peer-review, the journals have no quality claim to make. Did you know that you can ask the relevant colleagues to comment on or peer-review your work before and after publication, and you can add them as contributors to the paper? So, you can write and share your work with colleagues and put it on the preprint servers. Libraries and universities will not waste money on subscription fees of closed access journals; you won't waste your money on open access fees; the funders will not waste public money and tax on paying for open access.

Making money from free labour is not a new concept. Even the most brilliant minds of our world have been slaves to the publishing industry, where the journal authors, editors, and peer-reviewers do the work and do not get paid. At the same time, the publishers sell papers through individual and institutional subscriptions. When they hear complaints, they offer discount or open access as a solution. In both open access and closed access, two facts never change 1. The publishers get the money all the time only the payer changes; 2. Those who have done the cognitive and intellectual work will never get paid.

It is not fair that you have to pay to publish your own work. It never happens in any other sector but science. It is expected that if you have spent your time, skills, and expertise on anything, you should get paid for it unless you are volunteering. Even if you are volunteering, you don't pay for volunteering. From the publishers' point of view, you do pay for volunteering in science!

Publishing with the traditional model is costly, too; the publishers usually need a website, submission and proofreading systems, and paid editorial assistants. Interestingly, the editorial assistants are more from LMIC to make the process cheaper for the publishers. The publishers also pay LMIC people to make beautiful PDFs from your manuscripts. They assign DOIs and keep the records updated, and finally, they index the papers in relevant databases so that people could find and read them. They also have a marketing department to advertise the products to the customers and find intelligent people for free labour. Everyone in the process gets paid but not those intelligent people.

Between your work and your audience, the publishers are extra layers to benefit and not contribute to the quality. It is possible to exclude the publishers. As I mentioned, it is possible to send your paper to peer-review and get a free DOI from preprint servers. The databases will eventually index preprints and make your work visible; some of these databases already do index preprints. You do not need tiny fonts and two columns to reduce publishers' costs; you can make your manuscript beautiful and publish it on a preprint server immediately with no delay.

Decades of abuse should end, and we, my friend, are the ones who will end this gradually.

Chapter 9: Living a Royal Life

If you have heard of Tolstoy, Hemingway, and Shakespeare, you would know that their job was to write and get a proportion of book cover price. Sometimes, the publishers were ordering new titles and were paying them their royalties to have ease of mind in terms of finance and focus on writing. That system works and continues to work up until today. People write books and receive royalties; they also write for magazines, newspapers, blogs, or guides to get paid. It makes sense and looks logical and acceptable, but not in academia.

You write and publish papers in journals or book chapter, but no one pays you. Not only that, there is something called open access journals/books for which it is you who write and who pays. It is costly, and more than more publishers are following that model. It does not make sense, but people do that because some think they have no choice. The catchphrase 'publish or perish' transformed into 'publish and perish'. Because of the pressure of academia on researchers for publishing and having citations, they have no choice but to publish to get the promotion. When there were a few journals in each field, it was considered hard to publish; publishing meant that you are an outstanding researcher. Things changed. Everyone can publish because there are enough journals in the quality spectrum; the universities also changed their policies and now focus on only top or hot publications. However, people continue to publish for no reason. It has become an endless effort with no positive outcome but wasting time and money.

On the other side of the road, there are readers of these published materials. The main customers of this academic literature are university libraries who pay billions of dollars worldwide to get a subscription to these journals. For open access journals, this is the grant funders, the universities, or the researchers themselves who pay. Considering that the journals do not pay royalties to the authors or peer-reviewers, or editors, the publisher gets all the financial benefits. They turn researchers' free labour into money and rip off the university libraries and grant funders.

There are better ways to publish the research for free and make it freely available for your audience at the same time. It is possible to identify the open access journals that do not require open access fee from the Directory of Open Access Journals (DOAJ). Some funders also have noticed this abuse and started establishing their own free and open access journals.

It is a wonder that academics do not stop this abuse. They keep writing and publishing even though it is not necessary or valuable. It is painful to see pieces that could be a free blog published as a letter in a journal. More painful is that the many researchers who are aware of the worth of their work do their best to get published in journals with the highest possible Impact Factor regardless of multiple rejections while they know that there are preprint servers that can host any research and datasets freely and openly.

The number of journals grows, and as soon as there is a new hot topic, the publishers start a new journal. You must expect to see more open access journals on global health, digital health, climate change, quantum computing, blockchain, and artificial intelligence. The established publishers have no problem starting new journals. It is probably through clicking a button and automatically inviting a few editors and then waiting for money flow. The story does not end there.

When you reach higher levels of expertise, it is time for you to write a book and share your knowledge with the world. You will either be invited by publishers to write a book or finish the book and then find the publisher. It is only at the end that you will realise that you will get paid only between 1-20% of the book's price, which would be after deduction of other costs. If you consider the time you spend writing it, you will have to see your therapist. In some cases, the publishers say that they are happy to publish your book through the open access route, so not only you will have to spend your time on writing it, you also have to pay for it to be published. Imagine you are a slave who works day and night for free without earning anything, and then your master tells you that you should pay for your food! If this is not worse than slavery, what is?

The best way to publish everything for royalties is through the publishers who pay the highest possible royalties; the best way to publish anything for free is through free open access journals that do not charge you or your readers anything. The best way to publish everything rapidly is through preprint servers; don't worry about the visibility in databases and indexing; many indexing databases are aware of the importance of preprints and are now indexing them.

Chapter 10: Conference

Beside the journals, we also have conferences. Not everyone can publish in journals, but it is much easier to make it to the conferences. The peer-review process in conferences is rubbish, and the paper either is being accepted or rejected; there is no revision or share of peer-review comments. If you have nothing to say or, do you can still attend if you pay.

Payment for the conference is your money flushed down the toilet. Most academics have noticed this, so if they go to a conference it is for fun, and that's why the conference organiser try to set up the conferences in places with good weather and attractive holiday locations! You wonder why. Everyone knows it has nothing to do with science. It is a holiday funded by the university or your public funding. At my first conference as a student, I was surprised to be in a conference with over 2000 attendants but only about 100 in the main conference hall. The man behind the tribune joked that we should take the location of the conference to the beach. The researchers attend the conferences for the same reason that the students attend the universities: to have fun.

If the conferences are held for the sake of science, they should be free, located in a globally accessible and affordable place or broadcasted on an accessible platform. I refer to a colleague who said, 'if I have something of value to say, I will publish it as a book or paper; why put my ideas at the risk of being stolen in a conference'.

The conferences soon realise that charging people for attending and presenting is not enough because they usually had limited time. Hence, they first extended the days to three or four days. It will make it a better holiday. Then they realise they can have more presenters and generate more money; they need to have several presentations simultaneously in separate rooms; of course, you have to colon yourself to be present simultaneously in two separate locations. If that's not enough, let's add a poster session and ask people to pay hundreds of dollars to come and install a poster, a thing that can be done online at no cost for a wider audience. Such commercial approaches created a clutter of conference zombies who go around but know no one to network or a presentation with learning points. Many attend because the attending on its own –

and we no other efforts or activities – qualifies you for Continous Professional Development points you need for your career promotion or professional development. Those who decide on your career progress support or hold such conferences; indeed, there are no commercial interests involved.

I often plan to enjoy the conference without attending, and I realised that it saves money and time, and I could network with the people through emails and video calls during or after conferences. It was also possible to follow the most exciting presentation on Twitter if they are not recorded.

Conferences are another money pit to waste your time and get your money. Be very careful not to attend them just because you have funding or because you can; until further notice, a conference is an academic holiday. I have attended over 200 conferences and checked them after twenty years to see their impact and outcome on my academic career. I learned some helpful information from each. This information was not useable for me at all; they were just good to know. The most important conference papers find their way to you in some form or another, and the rest remain only as conference abstracts. I made some connections, including the international ones that did not end in scientific collaboration mainly because of the geographical distance, finance system in the universities, and strict grant application eligibility criteria that do not allow the international experts to apply for funding. In the end, what was left were photos from lunches, dinners, and the holiday part of the conference. So, the next time you see a conference, plan your holiday and buy your swimming suit.

Chapter 11: Citation Index in Stock Market

At some point, someone had an idea that citations can indicate how great you are. Scientists were the first selfie-takers, and self-citations history is way ahead of selfie and selfie sticks. The citation became a currency to show your scientific wealth. Following the stock market model, it was time to introduce indexes: Impact Factor for the journals, which became equal to the value of stock for investors; and H-Index for researchers stock, so you know if this or that researcher worth the investment. Such indicators are also something you need to declare in your promotion, job, or grant application. I suggest you put the following middle figure from your Google Scholar profile in your application for promotion and call it Finger 3.

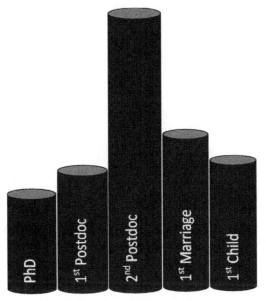

Finger 3. Number of Citations Per Career-Life Stage

It took decades for the researchers and the universities to realise that all these indicators are rubbish and even publishing them sends a wrong message. Who cares? Those who had better Impact Factor or H-Index keep rubbing them on your face and supporting these indicators; these researchers and journals are similar to the investors who invest their time and money on a stock and see it sinks in front of their eyes; however, they still believe that the stock can survive it. Who is responsible for all the times that the researchers spend on writing and revising the papers to get citations?

Those investor/researchers who were smarter focused on co-authorship on projects with the potential to receive citations. With little time investment, you can have a profile with hundreds and thousands of citations. You can agree among yourselves to cite each other's work. Some universities encouraged their scholars to have a Google Scholar profile to show off and cite fellow researchers from their institute. The journal editors also pushed authors to cite the papers from the target journal and subtly rejected the papers citing the competitor journals. This self-citation extended from the individual level into the continental level. USA researchers started to cite USA papers, and Chinese researchers continued to cite more Chinese papers. The journals subtly reject the papers based on unwritten prospective citability criterion – call it hotness or sexiness – to save and increase their Impact Factor regardless of signing DORA. This game of citations will continue for the decades to come. The purpose of the academic research became to get citations. Resistance is futile, and you must accept the reality before entering academia.

Sadly, in most countries, still, there are criteria related to citations or derived indicators from citations in promotion or grant application forms. The researchers are spending their life on writing hot but not necessarily valuable papers to get more citations. Review papers are now more important than research for getting more citations, and the researchers have shifted from laboratory to library research to review the literature inside their EndNote libraries. The academics had moved back to when they were students at school and the university writing essays, but this time it is called a review paper, not an essay. The is one more thing you will learn writing a review paper: the art of stealing. As Mizner said: "If you steal from one author, it's plagiarism; if you steal from many, it's research".

Of course, that citations like any other numerical data could be used for research, finding trends, discovering histories, and identifying emerging areas of science and so on; however, being used as an indicator to evaluate people, journals, organisations, and countries is an abuse.

One of my colleagues put it this way that 'if I had a dollar for each citation, I could have a house right here in my town in Florida'. He has worked 24 years in the same university and still pays the rent despite having 270,000 citations. Think again.

Chapter 12: Peer-Review

As soon as you publish one paper and your email address is visible for abusers, you become vulnerable to peer-review requests from the journals. They expect you to dedicate hours of your time (=money) and skills for free to the journal's quality and receive nothing of value in return. That's even more harmful when you realise that not only are they selling the result of your work either through journals' subscription fee or open access fee, but also their abuse continues to occupy all your free time in the future through invitations to peer-review. Congratulations, you are a voluntarily part-time abused academic. Your name will not be mentioned anywhere of value. Sure, Publons, but if you add your Publons record on your academic promotion application, no one will care because your institute will care about things you are doing for free for the institute, not the wealthy publishers. You take your peer-review records to Sainsbury's or Walmart, and they will not give you a pack of crisps/chips. You are doing it for science! You don't need money; you don't need food on your table or a life. Science will be enough for you.

Come on! Do another peer-review, show that you are an expert. How exciting!

Some journals started offering 10-20% off on open access fees for peer-reviewers. But to get that discount, you still must pay 80-90% of the open access fee! I negotiated with one of the well-known journals that I am happy to peer-review five papers and collect 20% discounts from all peer-reviews to publish one paper for free. Their answer was obvious: You are clever, but no, instead publish five papers with the journal, and eventually one will look free because of 20% you save from publishing each paper!

Reject all peer-review requests or remain a cheap scientist. Ask a surveyor to survey your house for problems and see if they are doing it for free. Ask a plumber to fix the flush for free or work around the house for one hour for free because they are experts in their field. If they don't, you should not peer-review anyone's work for free. You have years of experience in the field, and that expertise should pay the bills. You should get paid for your time like any other occupation or profession.

You would think that the peer-review is good, but as someone who has seen over 500 peer-review comment sets, I tell you that you need a re-think. The peer-review is too subjective, and when you submit a research paper to a journal, it is already too late to change anything. The research is done, and the funding is finished. You can clarify and add limitations, but you cannot change methods or results. The changes are going to be minor. If your paper gets rejected, it is not for scientific reasons; I think we can agree that you can publish any paper in journals nowadays. The main reasons for rejection are the editor or editor-in-chief's opinions on the quality of the paper and the journal's scope. Let me put it this way, would Science, Nature, or Lancet publish a paper with prior knowledge that it is not going to be cited at all within the next 5-10 years even though it is on an important topic? The journal, after all, is a media. Imagine turning on the TV, and the news reporter says that millions of children played today, millions of people ate today, and thousands of babies got born today. Would you watch the news? No. you need something exciting and different even though it is negative. The journals are no longer 'academic'; they are just another media looking for an audience.

Peer-reviewers are people who have no idea how productively they can use their time, and they prefer to spend it on spotting your typos. Their comments depend on their personality, the quality of their day and mood, the level of physiological and psychological satisfaction and so on. If they had a fight last night, you would pay for it. There are also two major types of peer-reviewers, those who hide and those who show themselves. In blind peer-review, they are not afraid to rip your paper up open, and in open peer-review, the same people become your best friend and an admirer. While there are many discussions on whether peer-review works or not, you need to reject all peer-review requests, especially the open ones.

Usually, the open peer-review is from open access journals, so either the authors are wealthy to throw their money into the toilet or from LMIC and are exempt from payment. In my experience, the review requests that you receive for open peer-review can last longer because you have to be very polite, or the authors will chase and hunt you down, physically or virtually. One of them offered me money to accept their paper in the second round. The second one begged me to accept research authored by a single person because he needed it to finish his education, and his supervisor was not signing the final form. He also said he wants to add his supervisor as an author, although the supervisor was not involved in that research. I contacted the journal to withdraw me as a peer-reviewer because I could not trust my clear judgement after his email.

All research should be out there for people, so see and judge and comment. Peer-review is very limited, and the only alternative is open post-publication peer-review which is fortunately possible with the free existing platforms. That would be true volunteering without involving the journals, their publishers, or commercial interests that affect all aspects of the current day's academic publishing industry.

Chapter 13: An Academic Beggar

With a PhD in hand, you finally become a postdoc and get your first position which is the same position you can get without a PhD, by the way. However, your salary will be slightly higher when you are a PhD, an advertisement-based salary, to say a PhD graduate gets paid more to encourage slavery. In reality, you can work full-time for three years, earned three years of salary, a PhD by published papers, and the same pay scale. But the universities will never advertise this path to you; if they do, they cannot abuse you for three years of PhD within the lowest possible pay scale. Well, now you are a researcher. Sorry, I offended you. Now, you are a scientist, is that better? Call yourself a research scientist because the researcher is too casual and unimpressive. Maybe a postdoc is even better. PhD was not enough. Stick to academia and do not let it go.

The little higher salary comes with strings attached to it. Now you need to learn the art of begging. It is called a grant application, and you apply for money to be paid into your university. If the grant's timeline overlaps with your full-time position, it means you are not going to get a single penny even if you are lucky enough to get the grant. All the money will go to the university to employ someone and pay them with the money you earned for the university begging. You will also feel horrible knowing that your kind and considerate line manager has begged for similar money to employ and keep you. They may have to continue begging to get your contract extended.

After a few rejections, you will notice that you are not getting the grant because you are not trusted even though your ideas are amazing, so you need to stand on the shoulders of giants to get that money. If they don't allow you to stand on their shoulder, you have to climb up their feet and hang from their testicles or breasts, or you will fall and fail. It sucks, and you suck until you rise above the testicles/breasts and reach the shoulders. Until further notice, you will be co-applicant on the grant. Since there is no way for the university to pay your salary forever, you must beg and find your salary and show the university that you are the best beggar. You may beg from a hundred people until one of them feels pity and toss a coin into your hat. An Uber driver earns more than you do, Doctor! By the way, do you like it when people call you Dr or do you find it offensive now that you are a skilled beggar?

At some point, you realised that it is not working for you and you need a permanent role. It means looking for a promotion. OK, so let's see what the criteria for your next step in the academic ladder are. If you want a promotion, you have to work for free for the university, so the university should earn money from your free labour for a few years and may or may not give you a promotion. The main criterion is the capability to bring money to the university through grants or students. It means you must share all your valuable ideas for free, hoping that someone will pity and award you a grant if they don't steal the ideas. But you are a beginner beggar, so in the best-case scenario, a single-digit per cent of applicants will get a few thousand for a project because you are just a PhD, 'early career' they call you. It does mean that you are not valuable because your value is dependent on the amount of money you bring to the university. You can be replaced by someone who can do this. It will usually take years to learn to be an intelligent beggar and get enough money for the university to offer you a permanent position. I always wondered why people invest all those years to get money for someone else, hoping and only hoping to get promoted instead of investing time in their work/life and getting money for themselves. It is a risky investment of time and money for a probable academic promotion.

That is just the beginning of slavery. When you know no one knows or cares about you and your tiny academic profile and a few citations, you have to go for testicles and breasts grabbing and let your line manager become the lead on your idea. At the same time, you do the leg work – should we call it leg job – and someone else gets the money, and another gets the fame.

Chapter 14: From Rupture to Raptor

Once I thought if I become a lecturer, my life will be easier because I don't have to beg for research money, and it is easier for a lecturer to climb on the academic ladder towards a professorship. There are always creatures who want a piece of paper called qualification. These creatures are called 'students'. The fever of university and college comes from Hollywood, just like the other solid ideas that we never question: you must get married; you must have children; you must celebrate Christmas. They are suitable for the benefactors such as governments and businesses who are funding these movies. Anything that costs is the topic of these movies. You need a wedding to spend years of saving to make sure you will never become financially independent; you must have children because we do not have enough human beings to ruin the earth and you know children cost, and the government need the balance between pensioners and workers or the system will fail, or God forbid, the country may have to accept immigrants to compensate the human resources. Finally, you need a few university degrees to waste your life and pay for them. All to do with paying. You should pay for a graduate degree and a master or a PhD as well. That would be at least seven years of your life that you will never get back. As long as this fever of higher education exists, lecturers will have jobs. So, it seems logical to have an academic career in lecturing.

Since we have enough stupid and incompetent people who need a degree to prove they are clever or good enough for a job, we will always have people looking for academic qualifications or pieces of paper that says: 'good dog!'. This paper shows that the beholder is stupid enough to spend three years on something that they could have learned online at no cost. Such a person is thinking-proofed and ready to be abused in the system for another three years of PhD for another 'good dog!' certificate. Being called a Doctor will satisfy part of their internal and external insecurity and incompetence and give them the confidence to apply for jobs.

I started asking my lecturer colleague if they enjoy two months of summer holiday and then realised that they are working overtime during the entire year. These universities employ a lecturer to generate between 150% to 200% of the lecturer's salary for the university. I was amazed when I noticed that supervising between 5-10 students on their projects will be enough for the salary of an assistant professor. Still, the university asks the lecturers to supervise as many as they can take and teach several modules and apply for grants and take PhD students and if they want promotion get a membership on university committees and do extra voluntary jobs and raise money for the University, and take the universities name into media and so on.

The assistant professors have more pressure on lecturing, supervising, and marking. You should add pastoral care to it because students' mental health suddenly became more important than the staff's mental health. The universities know that any investment in anything is a new cost, so the best strategy is to push things towards you in a more friendly way. When a new idea/policy comes around that requires you to do more work, the university will have training and workshops to clarify and explain and 'understand' your concerns and listen to you and engage and involve you in decisions that have already been made. They ask for your feedback and revise the plan. While there is no real person's name on such policies, they gather you around to comment on a room so that if you disagree, they will know and exclude you gradually. If you comment anonymously, they can easily exclude your comments, and if you complain, they would know it was you with those anonymous comments. There is no runaway; you are stuck with more and more work coming towards you. After years, you also are afraid, the same fear that every Abused has when they decide to leave their Abuser: 'What would I do if I leave? I have only been trained to do this'. You prefer to stick to your 'permanent' job.

I realised that lectureship is another form of slavery unless you are smart enough to unethically abuse the resources you have, just like the university does: the students. Students have dreams, and it is easy to abuse people with dreams. The emotional starry-eyed creatures who are here to change the world while they could not even change the pre-designed life pathway pushed them into the university.

When we were at primary school, we had a teacher who never was in the mood to teach or mark the papers. He outsourced all his job description to two of his students, including myself. We were teaching and marking the papers on his behalf. Since we were caring about the performance of our classmates and had a fear of 'see you after school' or 'let's take it outside', we were extremely fair in our teaching and marking, treated some students more equal than the others. Still, we were working with weaker students so they can catch up. It went well. While we were doing it for free and gaining teaching and marking experience, our teacher enjoyed his cigarette and salary. He knew the system so well.

There is a reason it is called 'higher education'; if you don't go to the university, you only had 'lower education'. 'Low' is not a very positive term to be referred to as: 'low-life'.

After five decades from that day, I have noticed that this trend continues in academia. The smartest of the lecturers have found ways around teaching: asking students to give presentations on topics of the lectures, or marking each other's works, or having activities; directing students to the books and papers rather than answering their questions; creating fewer slides and talking more; referring the students to YouTube videos; inviting PhD students or interns to lecture or supervise and so on.

While I hear the lecturers moan that the student outsources their essays, I found some lecturers from top universities also outsourcing their marking on online temporary jobs platforms. In another case, one of the lecturers asked me to log in to the university system and mark the assignments without reading the project reports. She said, 'as long as your mark is 15% different from mine, it is OK'. Some universities enforce a dual-marking scheme to be fair to the students without care about available staffing resources. The university's priority facing overload is to use the existing free human resources, divert the extra tasks towards the staffs, or abuse their love and enthusiasm. This philosophy turns those in the system into systematic abusers.

One lecturer confessed that he had to work with no interruption because of the pressure of deadlines in marking and quality control of the marks by a second marker. He forgot to eat or drink or go to the toilet on time. As a result of this continuous pressure, he ended up with acute constipation and got an anal rupture. That was the day I classified these lecturers as Ruptured Lecturers. He was raped by academia.

I think all lecturers start young and with high levels of energy and enthusiasm. They start from the 'Ruptured Lecturer' level, and it ends with 'Raptor Lecturer'. The latter class of lecturers hunt down any active students and abuse their energy and enthusiasm towards the lecturer's goal, which is probably a promotion. Finally, they get the academic freedom they deserved. When the university does not give you enough time to work on your ideas, you have no choice but to follow the university's pattern and abuse the existing free resources for the love of academia.

Chapter 15: A Recorded Webinar

Although some of the universities were already offering remote courses, recording the teaching sessions and webinars became more and more popular during the pandemic. What happened was that the universities noticed that many students would realise that they can study from their bedroom without attending or paying the university. Academics also realised that they were wasting all these years going to the university and teaching the same materials repeatedly. So, universities made an abusive case of recording the sessions and webinars. The problem was that there were lots of grey and undiscussed areas here. For example, how long the universities are going to retain the recorded lecturers? Did all lecturers and students consent to be recorded? And was the recording part of the academic job descriptions? Who owns the intellectual property of the recording? Can I upload my recordings into my YouTube channel, get followers, put ads and start earning money from them rather than lecturing in the university?

As a result, some of the academics wisely declined the request to record, some left the academia when forced to record, and some sold their heart and soul; they said they belong to the Abusers to be used in any way they want. One of my colleagues was pissed when she noticed her recorded sessions are being used in the university three years after leaving the university because there was nothing against this use. We are not lawyers, and we cannot afford one. Can we now sympathise with the rape victims?

While the production of these materials requires a massive amount of efforts, the universities did not pay anything to academics. While these recordings were as important as books, there was no royalties or copyright statement to protect the academics. Any materials produced by the academics when they are an employee of the university can be claimed as the universities' intellectual property. For branding purpose, the universities encourage the researchers to use a specific template for their materials, including slides and even their email signature. In all cases, the templates include the university logo.

Maybe it is time for free-thinking academics to start their own YouTube channel before it becomes illegal based on the new policy from the university. Think twice before pressing that recording button, and thrice before sharing the link or the video. Does it pay your bills? If not, it pays someone else's bills and luxury holidays.

I thought to write a separate chapter about the patents, but I thought the similarity would bore the audience. The universities consider the intellectual property of your work to be shared between you and the university even though your thought may not have anything to do with the university or its equipment. Since your salary from the employment in the university gives you financial security and free mind to think, whatever you think. Whenever you think, the result will be shared with the university. I have seen researchers who had to leave their academic career to save the intellectual property of their invention or idea for themselves.

Chapter 16: A Clown at the University

All researchers and lecturers in the university were invited to participate in a series of workshops on how to go on media, what type of research goes on media, and what resources exist in the university to help you 'disseminate' your research.

When people were interested in something, they would read a book about it in ethical days. If they wanted news, they were getting the newspaper. Nowadays, everyone is on social media, and everyone thinks they have something worthy to say or show or do and record. Everyone is a media, and the university asks you to tweet! You should create a Twitter storm and report the number of your followers and altimetric in your annual appraisal. I could not help noticing a very prestigious professor who was never seen out of tie to dress as a clown and make children laugh on TV to secure a tenure track through a few hundred thousand followers. The meaning of totally academic activities has changed. With the introduction of Hollywood as the popularity role model and the stock market as the business role model, we only bring up Capitalist-Narcissists in academia. Everyone holds webinars and seminars and begs people to participate; that's 'impact'.

It is not limited to research. The lecturers who bring free chocolate and coffee into class for their students and make them laugh are being ranked higher in student feedback and have a higher chance for a stable job and promotion. When planning your session delivery, you should think more about the jokes, not the academic content itself. It is the student feedback that matters. One of my honest students said that she felt ashamed when she saw a respected lecturer's breakdance to make people laugh and give him good feedback because of that dance, not lecturing software engineering.

The university asks the lecturers for more and more to give each day, and it involves being friendly and smiling and attractive to attract more clients (students=money) for the Abusers. One of the lecturers goes to the club with students and supply them with Cuban cigars. Another one had a birthday party and invited her students to drink until morning; I only knew when one of the students passed ibuprofen around my class, and I asked why. The purpose of the universities is to earn money. Science is secondary. Learning is there, but its pragmatic outcome regarding the job market is obscure.

Academics are friendly clowns who go the extra mile for the set goals.

Chapter 17: Supervisor

Supervision is fun and addictive. Those who design the academic systems are aware that academics are passionate, and perfectionists and science is addictive; therefore, it is the best place to abuse such passion and addiction and make people work for free. Supervision is another way of training but more one-to-one. It is very time-consuming if you want to do it right, but it is simple to provide supervision worth the value of the salary you receive. The problem is that there are no boundaries and some supervisors end up re-writing the students' work and spending too much time on their project. Eventually, the project gets marked and gets thrown into the bin. All those efforts for nothing.

If you decide to supervise, you should consider choosing the best students for yourself and ask for an output that lasts beyond the project's age. If not possible, there is no point in supervision. In the rest of the cases, the student wants a mark, and you want them to go away and not waste your time. It seems like a good negotiation if you give them a good mark only if they don't bother you. If you go easy on supervision, the university will expect you to supervise more students until you have no free time/life left or found dead behind your desk. Don't worry; it is not slavery; remember to think about passion and science and changing the world.

I need to point out that at the time of writing, one of my British colleagues shared a job advert with me from a UK university that looks for people to supervise undergraduate and postgraduate students, 20 hours (£360.80) per project. It is £18.04/hour before reduction of tax and pension and the other reducible costs. The students are usually happy to pay triple that to get their desired mark. It is not always about the bribe; one of my students contacted me after graduation and said that she was not satisfied with her supervision on the project and wants to repeat a similar project and offered me an hourly rate of 80$ to supervise her. I passed the request to one of my junior colleagues, thinking that this rate is the actual amount they were paying the university; however, because lots of hands who provide services and create bureaucracy and paperwork also need money, there is only £18 left for the supervisor. In addition, the universities provide other costly services such as paying their share in pension and access to library resources and databases, which is usually very costly. The low pay rate and unpaid overtime are usually the main reasons that cause job dissatisfaction and burnout, which leads to mental health issues. At some point and depending on how much people can take, some will see no choice but to find an alternative and leave academia.

The students are becoming more intelligent as well. They don't waste your time with projects; they outsource it to someone who knows how to do things. In some universities where attendance is mandatory, the students pay someone to sit in the classes on their behalf. The students are there to get the qualification, nothing else. If you wonder why some students don't need supervision, they are either self-learners or pay someone else to deliver.

As a supervisor, I have noticed that some students do not show to be bright deliver outstanding projects. When you ask them about their assignment face-to-face, they usually have no idea. However, if you communicate through emails, they will have time to ask the person who conducted the project for a fee.

Chapter 18: External Examiner

When for the first time, an extremely prestigious university contacted me to be an external examiner on a PhD thesis, I was thrilled. Finally, someone noticed I am the best. I am a peer. I am a reviewer of a thesis. I accepted and spent about 2 hours on paperwork and filling forms. Finally, the 580-page thesis arrived. I read it eagerly and loved it. To save time for the poor student, I prioritised it for my weekend and worked extra during the week and evenings and mornings outside working hours. In total, I spent about 60 hours on that thesis, plus 4 hours on the train, plus 2 hours on the viva voce examination and an hour to finalise the decision. Of course, I had to check the revisions for another 3 hours and accept them. Then wait. After two months, I received my travel expenses and £240 for 72 hours of working as an abused academic. That is what I deserved, £3.33/hour. The rate is how much twenty years of dedication to science worth. My child earns more than that doing errands around the house. That was the day I decided not to do any external examination and went internal-only if it is part of my job description.

An examination is just like a peer-review. The main difference is the volume of the work. A journal manuscript will not exceed 50 pages, but the thesis can be hundreds of pages, and that's why you get paid generously.

Several things also pushed me to decide to give up on external and internal examinations. In all cases, I realised that there is no point. You will not create an enemy who would key your car for a few decades, so you better say that it is impressive work and beyond PhD and all sort of crap. Leave along you may face their supervisors for the rest of your academic career, and they also can do the same to your student. Finally, you end up asking for a few revisions. This is called constructive criticism.

Chapter 19: Prestigious Esteemed Journal Editor

When you hear the word 'editor', you'd think it has something to do with 'editing'. Well, it is not exactly editing but about choosing pieces for the journal. We have several types of editors, and they do not edit.

The editor-in-chief is the highest one who usually puts the issue together and manages to get new editors and get rid of the 'inactive' ones. They also contribute to the policy and scope of the journals. Unlike democratic systems, this role is a dictatorship. Once one becomes an editor, they won't let it go because it is considered prestigious and shows you are one of the leaders in the world. It usually has no financial return. You spend your time so that for your time, someone else gets paid. That is called voluntary slavery. Some accept this role only when they retire, others just want to be king and stay a king, but since we do not have many kingdoms worldwide, they have to be convinced to rule a journal.

Some editors serve on the editorial board. They may discuss the manuscript among themselves and choose them for peer-review or reject them. In some journals, these editors also can invite people to write a review on a topic or invite reviewers to peer-review the papers. In journals that care about mass production and earning more money – mainly open access journals – associate editors are responsible for finding peer-reviewers and begging them to peer-review.

What editors do is being compensated by the appearance of their name on the journal's website or preliminary materials of the journals. The entire editing and journals system is copied from the same system from the newspapers. There is one significant difference, however. Everyone who works as an editor in the newspapers gets paid. Even the writers (authors) are being paid royalties for their works if acceptable for publications. If you remember Breakfast at Tiffany's, that's how Paul could offer to buy the silver telephone dialer.

If you can see the difference, you would know that the publishers are abusing the academics. There is no financial benefit in editorship and if you want to volunteer, make sure to volunteer where the world needs you the most. Many retired professors can start a free journal online and receive, review, and publish. You don't need someone to abuse science.

If you are an editor of open access journal, you must know that only the rich and poor can publish in those journals. Most researchers are in the middle. Most of the money that open access journals get comes from public funding or people's tax money into wealthy publisher's pockets.

If you are an editor of subscription-based or hybrid journals, ask your university libraries to see how much the university pays to access your efforts.

There is only one way to volunteer in the journals for free, and that is to help journals that are free for the authors and the readers; and yes, we do have such journals (See the chapter on open access).

You would think that being an editor is an important job, but it is not. You receive the manuscript, and in almost all cases, you send them for peer-review. The only part that involves your knowledge expertise is to find peer-reviewers who are experts in the topic. Then you send them reminders, and you receive comments from peer-review and send them to the authors and then receive the revised manuscript and send it back to the peer-review, and if peer-review approves, you suggest it as accepted. This process is repeated for almost 90% of all papers in open access journals because they just want to publish and get the money. In other journals' cases, the editors may reject more because they want the top and hot papers to make the journals attractive and raise the Impact Factor and make the journal look important. Other than that, the editor's work is what administrative staffs do and does not require much expertise. All editors could be replaced, which makes them free – I wanted to say cheap, but they are not cheap; they are free.

One of my colleagues showed me an automatic system that manages the mechanical processes from submission until acceptance without human involvement. A publisher has a system that can identify, rank, and invite the right peer-reviewers and editors to the editorial board. This publishing system has some journals with impact factors between 5 and 12, a dream for many editors. The system does not charge for open access fee in the first few issues until the journal gets an Impact Factor or indexing, and then it starts charging people. It is an auto-profit-generation system, and the majority of the authors or editors are unaware of the behind the scene. The journals also have a convincing list of editors on the editorial board. Out of curiously, I contacted three editors from three different countries. They said they have not edited or received a single paper and accepted to be an editor because the journal promised they only need the editors' names on the website, not their time. All the editors have automatically received a signed beautiful certificate that approves their editorship status for three years. The entire process of submission until acceptance is automatic without involving humans. Then the authors pay, and cheap human labour makes a beautiful PDF of their manuscript for them.

These things happen when academics welcome abuse.

I resigned from the editorship of six journals and left the editor-in-chief role from another journal. After working for free and publishing over 30 papers for open access journals, and encouraging poor peer-reviewers to peer-review for free, I realised that I had benefited the publishers over £50,000. That was after excluding the papers from LMIC. They offered me a 10% discount on publishing research and 20% on review papers, which means you also pay but a little less than the others. They also said that you would be on top of your field and up-to-date and all sort of rubbish. Being editor of a journal is another way of slavery. The publishers earn loads of money from your work and pay nothing back. Resign and save you hours for yourself.

Chapter 20: Invited

This was another way of generating income. If you are esteemed, you may be invited to have a free hotel room and free food to share decades of your knowledge for free. That's how much you worth. Not only that, your fans will pay to the conference to be there to see your live performance on stage, by which I mean your valuable speech. Since they may get bored, you also have to prepare some stand-up show jokes, totally who you are, a clown. They will enjoy and rate you highly in their feedback. Anything for science.

If you are in academia, you will be invited by strangers to do something. Deleting the invitation emails or marking them as spam is part of the daily tasks of every academic. Call for papers, call for chapters, call for presentation, call for the editorial board, and so on, all of which have something in common: no money for you. Even if they come from prestigious conferences or journals, the purpose of these calls is to use you. In all cases, you have to consider your benefits. Some of these calls invite you to submit a paper to a conference or journal, and then they ask you to pay; others say they are free for you, but then they sell your paper and pay you nothing.

When you see the next invitation, translate it as rape.

If you are a top researcher, you don't need to beg to prove it, you don't have to fill pages of evidence to ask for a promotion, and you don't have to work in the university. If you do so, it is because you are not a great researcher. If being a great researcher was important, the government should have supported them with a lifetime salary and asked them to think and conduct research on whatever they want and not on whatever the government needs. As a result of governmental needs, we have the most advanced weapons, but we cannot supply clean water to the world. The funding for developing weapons is secure and never stops, but to get funding to find cancer treatment, you have to apply and compete/beg for a limited pot of money.

Either you are an invited lecturer in a top university or an invited speaker at a conference. Your university does not care because it does not create income for the university, so it has nothing to do with your promotion. Recognition is good only if it directly or indirectly gets money for the university.

Long story short, the system is broken, and it is not going to be fixed by us; the abused academics have no chance or power to fix it. What they can do, though, is not to support such a system and prevent more abuse.

If you have something valuable to say, say it on YouTube and let the audience see and hear it with no time and place limit. You don't have to wait for being invited; you are invited every day by your logical mind to change the world through your thoughts, your behaviour, and your words.

Chapter 21: Chartered Member

J oining the societies and associations is another way to rip off the academics. Separating a few accreditation-related memberships in some fields such as medicine, law, or engineering that you must have to practice in your career, the rest of the memberships are scams and rip off. They just don't pay off. Just think about what you get for your membership fee, and if it does not worth it, just cancel the membership. Those societies need to learn their lesson.

The methods that such organisations use is simple. There is a common interest or sub-interest, and you can abuse that. They establish a society or association, or institute and offer membership for a fee. To make that fee acceptable, they list benefits for membership, which is globally identical: 1. They publish a newsletter for you; 2. You can apply for awards and grants; 3. There are training and workshops with a discount for your professional development; 4. There is an annual conference, and you will get discounted registration rate; 5. You can apply and pay for professional registration so that you can add another abbreviation after your name.

There are tailored pricing for membership so everyone with any level of income can be ripped off. The idea follows the journals' tiered subscription model with more scrutiny. For some people, it worth paying the membership, but for many, it never pays off. This practice also is different in every country. You cannot apply and get relevant jobs in some countries if you are not a member of such organisations. In some others, they only receive the membership fee and provide no benefits.

Such organisations should usually fight for the profession's rights, keep the employed people relevant to the profession and prevent non-professionals from practising the profession that requires high levels of skills. They should be powerful enough to negotiate and accredit the relevant employers and universities that train the professionals and disqualify those who do not follow the protocols. In most such membership-based organisations, this is not the case. They are there only to get money. When it comes to the university teachers, researchers, and students, there is no organisation to support them. The majority of such jobs are skill-based and not qualification-based. Some can become researchers or lecturer without a university education and through pure training and practice. So, it is just unclear why the first and the second classes of jobs and even the third class of academic jobs should join such organisations.

Chapter 22: Promote Yourself

I could not find any logic behind the application for promotion. How blind a university should be not to see who should get promoted and ask the academics to apply or beg for being rewarded. Why do you want to get promoted filling all that paperwork anyway? Filling a job application form is much better, faster, and easier. Apply for a higher salary job and get it. Then ask for your current institute for a price match and if they don't provide it, just leave.

What is to consider is not to be fooled by two factors: 1. Job Title and 2. University's Name. In my decades of academic life, I noticed that employers trick you into the jobs giving you better titles. For example, instead of secretary, they call you Senior Office Manager. The trick is the same with research jobs. For example, they name you a Senior Research Fellow, but they pay you as low as a research assistant. Famous universities are using another dirty trick. If the university is from among red bricks or ivy league, they will pay less for the same job that other universities pay way more. They know that some people will apply for those jobs to be part of a famous university and use their affiliation and email address; this allows their historical abuse. On such occasions, those who care about their affiliation will sacrifice their salary to show off their affiliation. In short-term, you may accept to work in certain places for a low salary to earn experience and skills, and in the mid-term, you may have to change your job from top salary to lower until you settle; however, the only accurate indicator that you are getting a better job and moving forward in your career in long-term is your salary.

Every year, each university decides to promote a percentage of the applicants to a higher level. Of course, this does not happen automatically by recognition. No one recognises you or cares about your work. You are invisible, and you have to show off and become visible and beg for promotion. You never get promoted for doing your job better than anyone else in the world. For such performance, you have your salary. Either you be a careful perfectionist or a careless, messy employee, the salary is absolutely and precisely the same. To get promoted, you need to spend thousands of hours from your own personal, family, and holiday time for a few years for the university. There are wide ranges of activities for 'volunteering' in the university so that the university makes sure that you can generate three times more than what they will pay you 'if' you get promoted. The thing is that if you generate the income that is equal to your pay raise after a promotion or even doubles that, you will not get promoted. Let's say you did all the free work for years, spent hundreds of hours for free and another hundred hours to fill the application form with supplied evidence of your devotion to your academic religion. Now, you apply alongside 300 other people. The university will promote only between 1-5% of the applicants depending on the university's financial status. Even though you might have created an incredible impact and income for the university, there are other criteria.

Being humble, you do your work, hoping that the work will make the noise. That's a good old days' strategy for granny; now, you get naked to win a Grammy. You must sing and dance and pave your way to the news. If you and your affiliation are on the news, that's called impact. That's the best advertisement for the university. You should be a media specialist and do the hot enough research to make the news even though it may not necessarily make the world a better place.

Even though you might be from LMIC who have worked their ass off and abandoned their families, friends, and memories behind for a better life and even though you are one of the bests in the USA, unfortunately, you are so humble, and you are not a coloured lesbian divorced single mom with two kids; that really will make a good news story and promote the university. If you are a big fan of diversity and inclusion, it is time to rethink what they mean in a promotional context. If you get promoted, the university cannot use you in the news to promote that it is an international university that cares about diversity and is not racist even though its bus drivers do not stop for international students and wait for white blondie to finish their phone calls before they hop on the bus. Well, you are a loser after all in this game. It does not matter how hard we try to push the system towards fairness; there will always be invisible minorities who will be ignored even though these minorities could be discovered in the following decades or even they can be a majority that has been overlooked. After decades, the universities may look back and decide that they have not been fair to their Muslim or Asian employees and put forward other policies. They may say that they have implemented the policies wrongly and overlooked minorities, and so on. But that will be too late, and you need to take care of yourself now.

I categorise here the promotions into two classes: Pay Raise Promotions and Permanency Promotions.

There is only one good way for pay raise promotion, and that is to apply to another job with a higher salary, and if you deserve to get it, you can ask for a price match from your current employer, or if you are bored, you can just go for the new job. Doing so, ignore the name of the university and the title of the job. Usually, the universities that do not have big names give you a good salary, a higher-level job and even permanency. Filling a job application form takes an hour, and you need a day to write a good letter. It is better than dedicating thousands of hours of your own time over the years and hundreds of hours on promotion application forms for something that may or may not happen.

The universities are already aware that the people may leave, so they do a proper evaluation to see if you can be replaced by someone who is more abusable than you. Until you wake up or find your way up, the university can make a profit.

The permanency promotion or some call it tenure track, goes through the Pay Raise promotions so that when you reach a certain level of the pay scale, all jobs are permanent. There you go. Remember that the universities, like any other corporate organisations, think about their profits; you should be your university. Applying for jobs is a full-time job.

Chapter 23: LMIC

Studying in low and middle-come countries (LMIC) has its own merits. For example, you will be surprised to know that many LMIC journals do not charge for open access publishing. Not only that, many LMIC universities will pay you if you publish a paper with their affiliation! On the other hand, the open access journals waive the open access fee for LMIC.

Academic abuse in LMIC institutes is not directly from the outsiders but from insiders. There is a broken academic system that mechanically copies the westerns institutes without considering the context. For promotion, you need papers, books, and citations. They are better to be written in English and the journals with high citation indicators. Not only you cannot write in English, but also you have no willingness or time to do so. Your students are the ones who can do it for you, so use them. Abusing students is widespread in LMIC universities, and there is nothing to stop the academic staffs from abusing the students. Since the students are dependent on their graduation and marks, which have been kept hostage by staffs, they have no choice but to nod to all requested from their lecturers and supervisors.

Some students work all days and nights for free for their supervisors; if they complain to authorities, their supervisors will know and take revenge. The authorities themselves are part of the same system that supports such behaviour. Not to forget, the students come and go, but the staffs are there. Unlike western universities, LMIC academic roles are permanent, and they are being paid directly through tuition fees or government and public funding. It is almost impossible to fire a lecturer or professor. That leads to proper dictatorship. These lecturers choose their replacement from among their loyal students and train them properly. This arrangement is no specific to LMIC; even in the USA, some departments do not employ young and bright scholars unless the senior lecturers are sure that they are getting a French maid to serve them until they retire; the right heir to the throne.

Sometimes the abuse continues even after the students leave the university. It is very usual for LMIC students to leave their country, hoping that they will find academic freedom in another country where the skills and expertise come first. Unfortunately, all jobs need references, and you have to put the most relevant references forward for recommendation letters – another hostage to take. There are several possibilities: 1. The supervisor writes a good recommendation letter and lets the student go (rare); 2. They never reply to the email that requests the recommendation letter because they are both jealous and see no benefit in replying to the emails (often); 3. The student contacts the supervisor and begs them for the letter and give away something in exchange for the letter or promises to continue slavery for the rest of their lives (usually); 4. Unaware of how academia works in the west, they write the worst possible recommendation hoping that student will not get the position and get back for more slavery (rare).

It is unfortunate that western universities are unaware of such abuse and keep asking for references for job and PhD applications.

Most abuse in LMIC comes from the higher levels of academics towards the lower levels of academics. For example, the lecturers and assistant/associate professors who look for a promotion use master and PhD students as their slaves to do the research and publish it or teach their classes. If you show that you are an active and passionate student, you will be in trouble because they will find and hunt you down so you can work for them for free. You end up having a long queue of guest authors on the papers, and sometimes your name will be removed from the papers, so you remain a ghost author. You don't get to choose your supervisor; they choose you like they choose their slaves looking in their mouth. You cannot complain because they have the authority to fail you. As soon as you graduate, you should run away to a higher income country or remain in the slavery system.

The wisest students stay quiet all the time, and they do not reveal their intelligence and interests. In some cases, they have to put down fewer efforts and intentionally try to receive average marks to stay hidden from the eyes of abusers until the right time to run away. When there aren't many prominent bright students in the class, the lecturers push the other students whose English is not as good. This practice leads to plagiarism, data fabrication, data falsification, duplicate publications, and so on that can easily ruin their entire academic career outside their country. Inside LMIC, there is no law enforcement for unethical practice, mainly because they are unethical but not illegal!

I have seen students who forge an acceptance letter or email for a paper to get the last signature and get graduated. Some of these students have established journals that provide acceptance letter in exchange for withdrawal letter to help the students graduate. So, the journal receives a manuscript that can be an empty document and issues the acceptance letter for today's date. In exchange and on the same day, the student writes a withdrawal request and asks the journal to withdraw the manuscript but dates the letter for one day after the acceptance letter's date. When the student graduate, the supervisor follows the paper but realises that the student has withdrawn the manuscript from the journal. This is, of course, the start of smarter abuses. For example, the supervisor may ask for published papers instead of an acceptance letter or take revenge from the student's friends who are now in junior years and could potentially be new hostages. The supervisors usually have an intelligence system to find your friends and track your publication record. If a student publishes a paper independently, the lecturers find out and make them pay. The practice is very similar to an oppressive political system.

When you get employed in such systems at higher levels, it is normal to have guest authors and be ghosts. As an unethical example, it is acceptable in many countries to have the head of the university, department, or centre as an author on all papers. Even the journals are aware that the listed authors have not done anything. One of my students showed me a paper and track record of peer-review for a paper, but she was not an author. When I asked why, she explained that the head of the centre said that the rest of the team are PhDs and she has a master's degree, and it is not suitable for the paper to have a master student as lead or even as an author. The paper was the report of her master's thesis that she was working on for two years and her thesis was the reason she was accepted for the PhD position outside their country. Her centre manager wrote in her recommendation letter that she is a selfless 'obedient' girl who makes sacrifices for science, and he hoped that they would work together in the future again.

Writing or translating books through the students is another way of abuse. The lecturers ask students to write book chapters and publish them as an editor to get the royalties and promotion. Sometimes they also remove the students' names from the chapters and replace them with their own Goodfellas. These activities are kept hidden; if revealed, there won't be any undesirable consequences. For example, the students think they are doing their coursework, and they never look back to see what happened. Unfortunately, there is no system to encourage the students to share their coursework freely and openly online after receiving the marks; if so, any abuse could be detected as plagiarism.

Another employee explained why his three-year full-time PhD took seven and half years when his professors realised that he is a fluent English writer. They used him as their own 'promotion cow'. He showed me how he had published two papers in top journals for each of his professors who became the lead and corresponding authors before they allow him to graduate.

The luckiest of the students are allowed to add their friends and classmates in the papers as authors, and they do this for each other so they could build a paper-full CV that helps them get a job or PhD inside or outside their home country.

The way the university lecturers behave with these students motivate the students to start a new and better department, and that's how the number of departments keeps increasing. Since they are all in a wrong system, after a while, the same goodwill turns into evil will when the graduates realise that in that system, you cannot compete with a professor that has thirty full-time students who write papers for him. Hence, you turn into evil eventually with an army of students who write and publish for you.

The bright side is that these students become strong because of such abuse and lots of work experience and possess many academic skills to quickly succeed when they enter western universities as student or staff. With restrictions lifted, they rise and shine. However, the fear and paranoia stay with them. When I offered one of them that he should be the first and corresponding author of the paper and I, as the supervisor, don't meet the authorship criteria, he burst into tears.

I must confess that not all professors in LMIC universities the same. The only way to find out about what's going on is to sit down with your international students and colleagues and talk about their experiences.

Unfortunately, unethical does not mean illegal. Even though such academic crimes have been illegal in some countries, other countries have copied only those aspects of the western universities that benefit certain academic groups and pave the way for their success.

Chapter 24: Ethical Academia

n terms of speed of progress and keeping up with the world, humanities – including ethics – is behind social sciences such as sociology and psychology. On their own, social sciences are yet to catch up with experimental sciences. The experimental sciences are yet to catch up with hard sciences such as engineering, physics and mathematics. Oddly, most people do not like two ends of this spectrum: Philosophy and Mathematics.

Ethics is a constantly updating field, but it is considered a branch of humanities. Ethics usually wait for the problems to merge before finding or suggesting a solution. Engineering is constantly making things better and putting out new stuff even though there is no problem to solve. The purpose of engineering is innovation and making new things or making old things better.

To highlight the gap, I give you an example. In experimental sciences such as medicine and pharmacology, when you find a new medicine that may be useful for 100,000 patients worldwide, it should go through a thorough process before entering the market. This process continues even after the medicine is in the market to find the rare adverse effects. This process usually takes between 3 to 10 years, and each medicine should receive approval from each country's authority before entering a new country's market.

Now let's go for engineering and technologies, Facebook, Twitter, YouTube, Nuclear Bomb, Cars, Planes, Mobile Apps. Should I continue? These technologies changed the life of billions of living creatures. None of these technologies went through any of the processes that medicine goes through before approval. They just came out, and people died, and they keep coming without permission from anyone. I must add using Artificial Intelligence now in every aspect of our lives. Grammarly corrects students' mistakes, and after twelve years, now people are discussing if it is ethical to use it. Google and Facebook abused our data for over a decade before EU regulations – known as GDPR – becomes mandatory. It took us a Brexit and a Donal Trump to realise these tech companies are the politicians who govern the world with purely commercial interests. Even when the websites had to ask your consent, they added Cookies that are now making things worse than before GDPR. You do not have time to read user agreements and change Cookie settings. Although having user agreements and Cookie notifications are 'legal' requirements, they do not necessarily meet the 'ethical' requirements.

Many websites do not have a 'Reject all cookies' option to stop them from gathering your information and sending you spams for the rest of your life. The separation of ethics and law adds to the problem and shows the gap that can only be filled through multi-disciplinary collaboration emerging from non-conflicted academia. These are examples to show you that ethics, just like other humanities, is always behind; governments or investors do not invest in ethicists because there is no financial return. Not only that, the entire world media – by which I mean Hollywood – positivise medical doctors and engineers and advocates living in the moment and lack of care about anything that does not immediately affect you. Carpe Diem or Mindfulness or living in the moment, they call it. Based on the media's description, the lawyers are people who suck your money, so the legislation is being delayed until a decade after the emergence of technologies. Ethicists yet to convince the people that Cookies are unethical, but Hollywood says who cares 'it is not like it's illegal or something'. In short, being ethical is not mandatory; it is an option that usually is expensive with less financial benefits; remember that we are living in a capitalist world, not an ethicist one. People tend to queue behind USA doors for citizenship; there is no ethical country to apply for citizenship, and if there is, they must be poor.

That's why we blame people who are killing each other on the other side of the world without questioning that they are using weapons – technologies – that our country makes and sells to them. For the same financial benefit, the world ignored climate change for decades because there was no money in it. Many believe that human civilisation and humanity is going to end by human being's ignorance in humanities. We are good at the rest of the sciences.

It is mainly Academia's fault that we do not educate everyone on ethics, and even if we do, we only focus on the parts that most people do not like, philosophy. Pragmatic ethics is missing from all courses, and the universities do not like to pay one more person to teach ethics. They should know about the theory of diversity and inclusion decades after the abandonment of slavery, but they should never know that asking foreigners 'where are you from?' is microaggression; maybe they will know within another ten years from now. If you want to attract students to a software engineering course at the end of the day, you should talk about software engineering. It will not be appealing for the students to pay a considerable amount of money for software engineering course and learn ethics. With the universities ignoring the most important academic education content, the responsibility falls on poor abused academics' shoulders to teach ethics without being paid.

Ignoring ethics in academia is not new; it is now decades that the social and experimental scientists show that 'people are difference'. You cannot shove thirty different people at the same time into the same place and give them the same materials and lectures and expect them to learn. Of course, you can do that to rip them off and earn money; it is unethical but not illegal; just like asking for more tuition fee from international students or asking for more work from employed staffs. People being different means that they need their own time and space for learning at their own pace. Therefore, I always tell my students to ignore me and my slides and materials. You will not learn anything in my classes; your learning will happen in your own time and place and outside the classroom.

The abuse in academia is under the pyramidical effect from top to down. The government subsidises education in the university. It pays for part of your education because they know that you will work your ass off to get a highly paid job, and so the government will get higher tax returns. The universities take as many students as possible and ask for as many tasks as possible from staffs. The main goal of the universities is to avoid or reduce costs and increase incomes. Education and ethics and all the other socialist and ethicist viewpoints are secondary and tertiary to capitalists. The only time that university talks about social science is when they try to encourage the sense of community and diversity through pictures in their adds and Student Unions who beg for a piece of their own money to be spent so that the students want. These unions control the pressure of riots by giving occasional tiny freedoms – an approach that has always worked.

From the university level, we come down to the divisional and departmental levels. Why do we have departments of X? Do we need all of them? It is a market selling qualifications, and it creates competition, but you must know how we ended up here. It is the academic-academia or Abused-Abuser relationship. Many who spend too much time in academia learn the skills to live and survive in academia; after a PhD, it becomes tough for them to return from the ideal world to the real world and face reality and usual people. These are the people who stay in academia because being academic is the only thing they know. If they leave the university, they don't know what they can do with their skills which are useless outside academia. So, they should stay in academia, but you cannot get employed if there are too many PhDs and only one department. In addition, many departments are exclusive and do not allow anyone new to enter because the fresh enthusiast lecturer may question all their traditional boring ways of teaching and out of date materials. The only way is to create another department that takes graduate students. The problem is that graduates would want the master's degree, which means creating a master's course, and finally, you will be a professor who supervises PhD, and these PhDs can go around and create their departments. That's how academia grows as the population grows. Again, this is not about the ethics. It is about you taking care of yourself without caring that how many years of beautiful young lives are being wasted until you get a salary on payday in your bank account; at the same time, others who do not know teaching or research receives a salary ten times higher than yours only through abusing you around the academia.

If you think it ends there, think again. If you are a lecturer, you will have students but do not look at them as students. They are now your employees. Now that the university abuses the lecturers, the lecturers find ways to abuse the students in the name of learning and education. They can read and summarise books and papers for you; they can teach on your behalf, they can set meetings and seminars, raise money for your research, write your papers, and it will all be for free.

They can be your ghost authors, and you can be their guest author. They will need your recommendation, will them not? So that's the only currency they will get, and they should work their ass off to deserve that payment. If you see an active student, take them as your student for supervision and convert their energy into another step on your academic promotion ladder. If you can find enough enthusiast, you can ask them to write book chapters, and you can become its editor and get the royalties. Think big, you know. Remember to smile and laugh and keep a friendly face all the time, so no one suspects you are raping them.

If you see people not citing your papers, reject them. If you are an editor and your competitor colleague who refused to employ you in their department submits a paper to your journal, reject it; even better, you can keep them in a loop of worst peer-reviews and waste their time and delay the climb on the academic ladder, anonymously. Don't employ bright students; that will decrease your popularity eventually. Stick to your academic chair until you die behind it. Be paranoid that people are there to take your leather chair and ladder steps. Fear their growth; they will smash you. Gossiping is not illegal; use it as a weapon to limit their network and delay their progress. They are young and will make mistakes, remind them of their mistakes and failures, and break their self-esteem and self-confidence. Use pastoral care as a weapon to learn about their secrets like a good catholic priest and use the darkest ones against them; then you can be mental health champion of the university for holding more pastoral care sessions than anyone else; two birds and one stone. Is it not enough?

Traditionally, mark for money/sex was the most apparent abuse, but it has become illegal and unethical. It was not like that all the time. A village teacher is still receiving chickens and eggs from the parents and considers the gifts in educating their child. The lecturers are being paid by their students in cryptocurrency for their marks now. It is not traceable, and in those cases that it is, it is very costly. Use all the approaches that are not against the rules and build your way up the way that the university taught you.

Teaching and preaching ethics will never be enough. We have to move from ethics to legislation that makes the right to abuse illegal in academia; until then, resistance against academia is the best we can all do.

Chapter 25: The Futures

There are more than one imaginable futures for academia. The future is collective of the moves that every single one of us makes right now. We are the future.

Virtual Universities

The most expected change is that most of the universities will present many courses online and remotely. Some of the courses can be delivered entirely online, and there is no physical attendance required. Some universities were already delivering Distance Learning modules and courses, and it is not something new.

Since it won't be possible for all the practical courses and sessions to be delivered online, many courses will turn into a hybrid model. You will attend the university only when needed.

There are so many benefits to going online that overshadow disadvantages. It is environmentally friendly, but it also saves costs for the students, staffs, the universities, and the government. The travel and office costs could be deducted from your education costs. The government will issue a visa or may accept some courses to be visa-free for international students. Everyone can learn without time and place limitations at their speed.

The disadvantages are that some student like the experience of being in an academic environment, and so hybrid classes with physical and virtual attendance will start this transition. The students can choose to stay at the university for a month and go back home for a couple of months. Such scenery changes will make life more exciting and out of routine.

Because of the possibility of recording the sessions, we should expect a reduction in the number of lecturers. Many lectures may be delivered by actors and actresses who can perform better than lecturers. There will be still need for a few people to update the materials or answer the questions.

Cryptocurrency

With the success of cryptocurrencies, universities will accept crypto payments for tuition fees. It will make it possible and more democratic for North Koreans to study in top universities without worrying about breaking economic sanctions imposed on innocent people. The government will not stop the universities because if they do, there will be new emerging universities with no physical location or dependency on any government who will employ the unemployed staffs of other universities to deliver the same courses and get payments in Dogecoin.

University of Internet

Many students who cannot afford the university or can afford it but think it will be a waste of three years of their life may decide to study independently and on the internet. As a result, the universities will experience a decline in their enrolment rates. It is expected that the universities will start targeting students of all ages, including pensioners, to keep up with the costs.

University of Industry

Many businesses and industries will have their training courses for candidates; passing them will qualify them for jobs or job application. It means you won't have to get a PhD to be employed at Google in your 30s. They will teach you what you need, and you can start your work when you are only 19 years old.

Fall of Un-Tops

Because of the lack of interest among the young generations in universities, we should expect downsized or merged universities. Many universities will give up their education sector and will focus on research only. Some of the universities will be closed forever. Like the fall of the Soviet, the other universities will try to get the best staffs of the failing universities to empower themselves and survive the future shock.

Consultants

At the early stages of the change, the universities will have no choice but to save money. Paying for pension and providing benefits for the staffs is costly. Using external consultancy and outsourcing the research and teaching will make more sense and remove lots of paperwork. Then the universities can focus on getting the money and students rather than managing human resources who strike now and then for pension and pay raise.

Humanities in Crisis

Because of the lack of funding, we will see fewer ethicists, humanitarians, and social scientists. They are rare even right now. While the law will remain hot for finding holes in registration for the companies to earn more money, the ethics will be merged into the existing courses and maybe abstracted into one or two slides. Personal benefits will overshadow public benefits; we should expect more cyberwars and civil wars between governments and the public, mainly asking for regulating the businesses and industries. The politicians are late as usual, and politics also is a sub-set of humanities that will suffer from the changes.

Services

With the technological difference, you will no longer need a laptop to install and run and save. The laptops will be dumb terminals that will connect to cloud-based services running all the required programs and saves them. Top tech companies will provide these services to all universities, and there will be no or little need for the IT department. As a result of automation, most of the admin works will be done by the computers. The computers can immediately inform the students if they lack a document in their application or if they have one day to submit their assignment. The systems will inform the students about their classes, exams, deadlines and all the things they need to know. Digital personal assistants will organise meetings and reply to emails. These changes will save the costs for the universities, but they may pay a bit more tax to the government so that the government could pay unemployment insurance for those who will lose their jobs.

Real Estate and Hospitality

Because of all the empty buildings and halls that the universities will be left with, it is predicted that the universities will enter the real estate business. The office concept is very old when people had to work with papers, folders, copiers, and printers. With the digital revolution, we won't need offices in the workplace. The universities will start either renting out the offices to other businesses or change their function into something useable. Because of the excellent location of the universities, some of the buildings could change into hotels and dormitories, and halls can become hostels for short stays. Who knows, maybe they finally open those spaces to homeless people to make a home out of it.

It is expected to see the universities opening shops in Malls and selling their branded condoms, potato chips, and notebooks, of course. Their hospitality business will boom when those who seek inspirations will be happy to pay a fortune to sit behind a Nobel Prize winner's desk or smell the pee from the bathroom that once they have pissed in.

Advertisement and Marketing

We should expect more professors on TV ads to show the authority of the products. Engineers will tell you how significant and safe the new bathroom flushes are, and the medical professors will ask you to attend the university after your 70s to keep your brain active and healthy. They won't be annoyed by such activities; they are already advertising the university on the news and their papers; this is scalable and pays the bills.

Antique Business

To attract both geeks and nerds, the universities will start making the collectables such as annual dolls, symbols, or anything with limited edition and availability. The scarcity will make them valuable and will earn money for the university. In the long-term, they will become precious items.

It is likely that with a lack of money, the universities will start selling their assets and buildings brick by brick. Those who have studied in those buildings will pay a lot to hold a piece of it. This antique business will continue until selling any physical thing left of the universities. To test run, the university can start renovating a building and selling the leftover rubbles on eBay to see if I am right. Volker Pawloski could build a business and retire with pieces of The Berlin Wall, which was a symbol of lack of freedom because of communism; now, the universities can do the same for the symbol of abusing intellectuals. The smartest of students take the pieces in advance and for free before they go on sale on eBay. Those who think earlier will benefit more; act before it becomes viral and illegal. Removing bricks is dangerous; go for cutlery and mugs.

Conclusion: Leave Your Dreams or Update Them

The university is not such a dreamy place; it is good enough for some but not for everyone. The problem is the Abuser-Abused relationship that does not let the academics go and change the world for good. They usually do not know what to do if they leave abusive situation. I am not here to give advice. I can just report my observations, and you can make a judgement on your own. Do your research and decide what you want to do. You may also decide to be connected to the university when your main job is not academic.

Industry

Many join industries even though you are not an engineer or researcher. I know an ethicist who works for an AI start-up to consider all the ethical aspects of their technology; for being an ethical technology, their business is booming.

Specialists: Your Own Boss

Some people start building a one-person business and expand it by doing work related to their speciality. With good planning, a workable idea, and online visibility, they may succeed.

Generalist: Multi-Potential

Some people can provide products and services for others, but they do more than one specific job. They have learned that they have skills in several areas and so can deliver several services. Driving for Uber and delivering for Amazon are some of the immediate thoughts.

Knowledge is Power

Some people negotiate with the industry and university and because of having specialized knowledge could have the universities and companies as their client and deliver services to them. In the future, it makes sense for many universities to outsource lots of works rather than suffocate themselves in paperwork, admin costs, and managing the human resources.

Capitalism-Socialism Balance

While the world is being divided between east and west, it is important to balance your financial capital and social capital. Although all Hollywood movies are encouraging and advocating the sense of community, socialising, and socialism, in the real world, you see more capitalism than any other 'ism'. Family and friends could be the best capitals and source of business and life support. If your parents can take care of their grandchildren, that will save a fortune for you. If they can help you build your business, you will be more comfortable with them than asking stranger abusers for help.

Private Teaching

It does not matter if you are a junior researcher or a professor; you can always find things to teach or create online courses that people can buy and attend. You can write a book about a topic and publish it with a publisher that will pay you maximum royalties. You can manage a YouTube channel that makes the world a better place without wasting people's time.

Idea

You hear crazy ideas every day. Someone collects money to live in a toilet for a year. Another one promises not to eat anything and survive by drinking beer for a year and live streaming it to collect money. One makes cute keyrings; another one invents one new food every day. The world is filled with ideas. Look at a few financial independence stories on how people turn a crazy idea into money and give it a try. In most cases, you don't have to leave academia immediately to chase your idea.

It will be your side hassle until you feel comfortable working on it full-time.

The Last Message

This book was a small step to have a different look at academia; this point of view is not being encouraged for being anarchist for the system; however, those who can think also deserve to get the rewards. I am not trying to convince you to leave the university. I am just trying to help you think and rethink and continue thinking and updating your dreams every day. If you decide to stay in academia, consider your ethical benefits; see what benefits you can receive from the university and what training is available for you; if you think you deserve a pay raise, ask for one or leave to a better job and salary. Say no to any request that does not pay you but makes money out of your free labour. We are not living in a fair world, and the regulations that will defend us may not be here for a few decades from now. It is up to us to let the abuse continue or put an end to it.